Alchemy
of Desire

DAMIANI

Alchemy of Desire

A STORY, A FAMILY,
AND AN ITALIAN PASSION

Edited by Cristina Morozzi

RIZZOLI
NEW YORK

New York · Paris · London · Milan

EDITED BY Cristina Morozzi

ART DIRECTION Sergio Pappalettera

LAYOUT Daris Diego Del Ciello and Gaia Daverio

EDITORIAL COORDINATION Sara Saettone

TRANSLATION BY Nadeem Abbas and Anne Kendall – Lsb Italy

EDITORIAL STAFF Ester Borgese

PRODUCTION Sergio Daniotti

PHOTOGRAPHS:
© Damiani Archives (2, 12, 15, 16, 19, 20–21, 23, 25, 27, 28–29, 31, 32, 35, 36–37, 39, 41, 43, 44–45, 47, 48–49, 51, 52–53, 56, 58, 61, 62, 65, 66–67, 68, 73, 74, 79, 82, 84–85, 86, 88, 94–95, 96–97, 98–99, 100, 102–103, 104–105, 106–107, 108–109, 110–111, 112–113, 118–119, 120, 124, 126–127, 128, 132, 134, 136, 138, 142–143, 144, 146–147, 148, 150–151, 152, 154–155, 157, 159, 161, 162, 164, 167, 168–169, 170–171, 174, 176, 178, 180, 182, 184–185, 186, 188, 190, 192–193, 194, 197, 198, 200–201, 202, 204–205, 206, 209, 210, 212, 214–215, 216, 218–219, 220–221, 222–223, 224, 226–227, 228, 230, 232–233, 234, 237, 238–239)
© Justin Arana (pp. 116, 120–121)
© Corbis (pp. 14–15, 18–19, 22–23, 26–27, 30–31, 34–35, 38–39, 42–43, 46–47, 50–51)
© Fabrizio Ferri (p. 93)
© Giovanni Gastel (pp. 6–7, 64, 69, 72)
© Getty Images (pp. 94, 106, 109)
© Dominique Issermann (pp. 90–91)
© Carlo Lenti (pp. 59, 130–131)
© SGP (pp. 71, 94–95, 96–97, 106, 109, 112–113, 114, 179, 189, 196, 208, 236)
© Claus Wickrath (pp. 140, 145, 149, 153, 156, 158, 160, 163, 165, 166)
© *L'Orafo valenzano* (p. 60)

First published in the United States of America in 2014
by Rizzoli International Publications, Inc.
300 Park Avenue South
New York, NY 10010
www.rizzoliusa.com

Originally published in Italian in 2014 by
RCS Libri S.p.A.

© 2014 RCS Libri S.p.A., Milan

2014 2015 2016 2017 / 10 9 8 7 6 5 4 3 2 1

ISBN: 978-0-8478-4283-4

Library of Congress Control Number: 2014930880

Printed in Italy

NINETY YEARS TOGETHER

Our father, Damiano, passed on his passion for the jewelers' art—the same that our grandfather Enrico had bestowed to him—to us. And it's this feeling of belonging that keeps our family team tied together—still affectionately ruled by our mother, Gabriella. Our family bond will always be a strong point. We support each other's choices, as only a family can do. We're linked by the harmony of ideas and the desire to pursue the same goals.

Our apprenticeships were special because we were lucky enough to learn the trade alongside our father, a visionary and talented man. We learned to transform a craft profession into a business, a business that we are still continuing to develop successfully today, expanding into international markets and giving jewelry production the added value of a recognized brand hailed around the world.

The
Damiani Ninety
Collection

ELEMENTI
LOGOMANIA
DAMIANISSIMA

NERV+

NON
RACCORDARE
TROPPO!!

The Damiani ninetieth collection is a limited
edition comprising ten pieces of jewelry,
each inspired by a decade of Damiani's history
from its foundation to date, created to celebrate
the company's ninetieth anniversary.
From gemstones to pearls, each exemplary piece
was created in nine numbered pieces to tell
the story of the company through the decades.

Charleston

The Charleston necklace gently encircles the neck, brushing the cleavage with a fluid pattern, inspired by the outline of a delicate feather. With almost one thousand diamonds, each of which is set one by one and which frame splendid pear-shaped diamonds of a higher carat—all carefully selected for shape, size, and color by expert Damiani gemologists. The fine pavé, illuminated by the diamond "drops," embodies the youthful works of Enrico Grassi Damiani and the soft forms of the Art Nouveau style.

A KISS ON THE HAND MAY MAKE YOU FEEL VERY GOOD, BUT A DIAMOND LASTS FOREVER.

ANITA LOOS

Gentlemen Prefer Blondes, 1925

Cascade

THE THIRTIES

Dominated by Art Deco style, the 1930s is captured by the imposing Cascade bracelet, with a jagged profile that evokes the stylized design of a waterfall, which reveals alternating black and white diamonds in movement. Using 623 black diamonds and 675 white ones, the Damiani designers and specialists spent months creating this splendid double-sided bracelet. The geometric design pays homage to the early works of Grandfather Enrico, destined to become the Belle Époque collection, which is still a Damiani best seller around the world.

DARE MOBILITA
ALLE FRANGE

Legend

THE FORTIES

In a difficult decade that intended to leave behind the aftermath of war, an austere fashion favoring military-style suits and coats asserted itself. Jewelry, with its full-bodied shape, also supported this new female image. The Legend bracelet is presented with a progression of wide bas-relief, highlighted by luminous lateral pavé in diamonds. Its magnificent semirigid processing, which is incredibly comfortable to wear, includes 264 white diamonds that are set upon jointed elements. It is inspired by a collection that Enrico Grassi Damiani had to produce in iron in the autocratic years, when gold could not be used—a highly successful collection, despite the times.

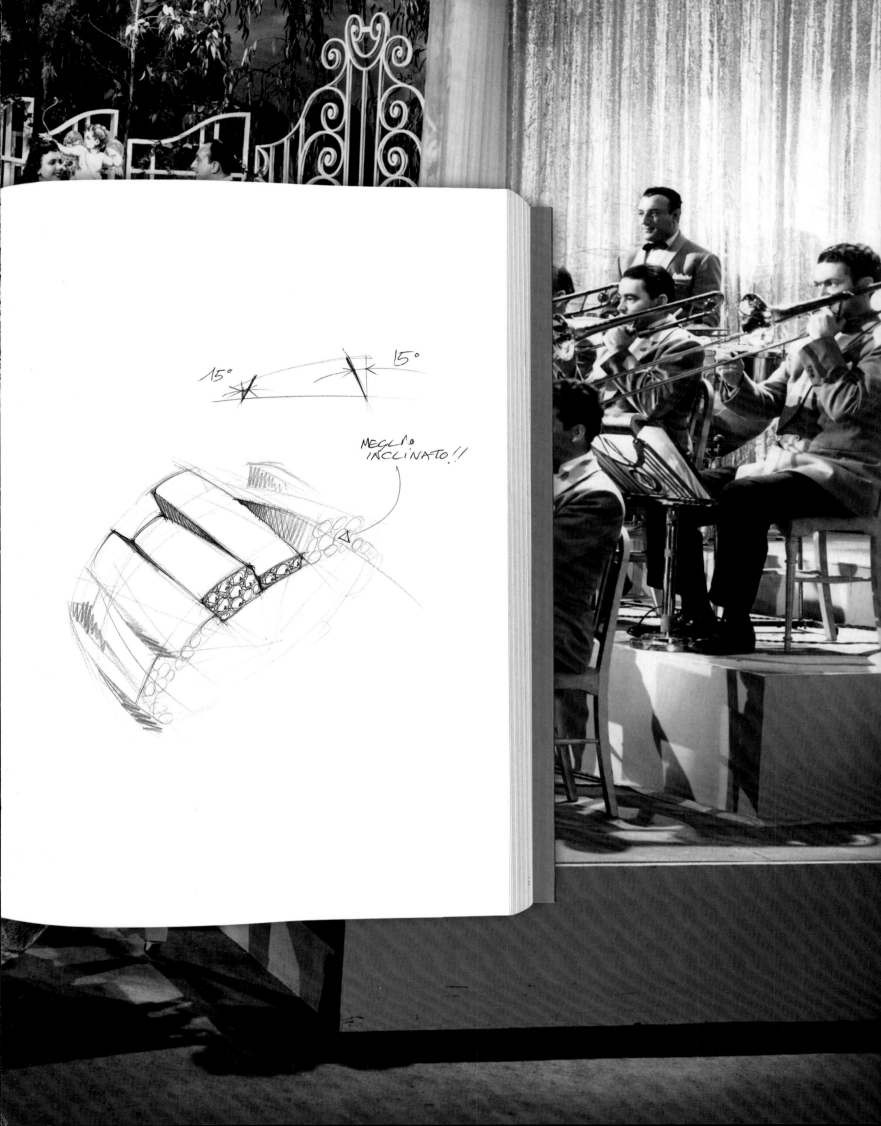

I NEVER HATED A MAN ENOUGH TO GIVE HIM HIS DIAMONDS BACK.

ZSA ZSA GÁBOR
The Observer, 1957

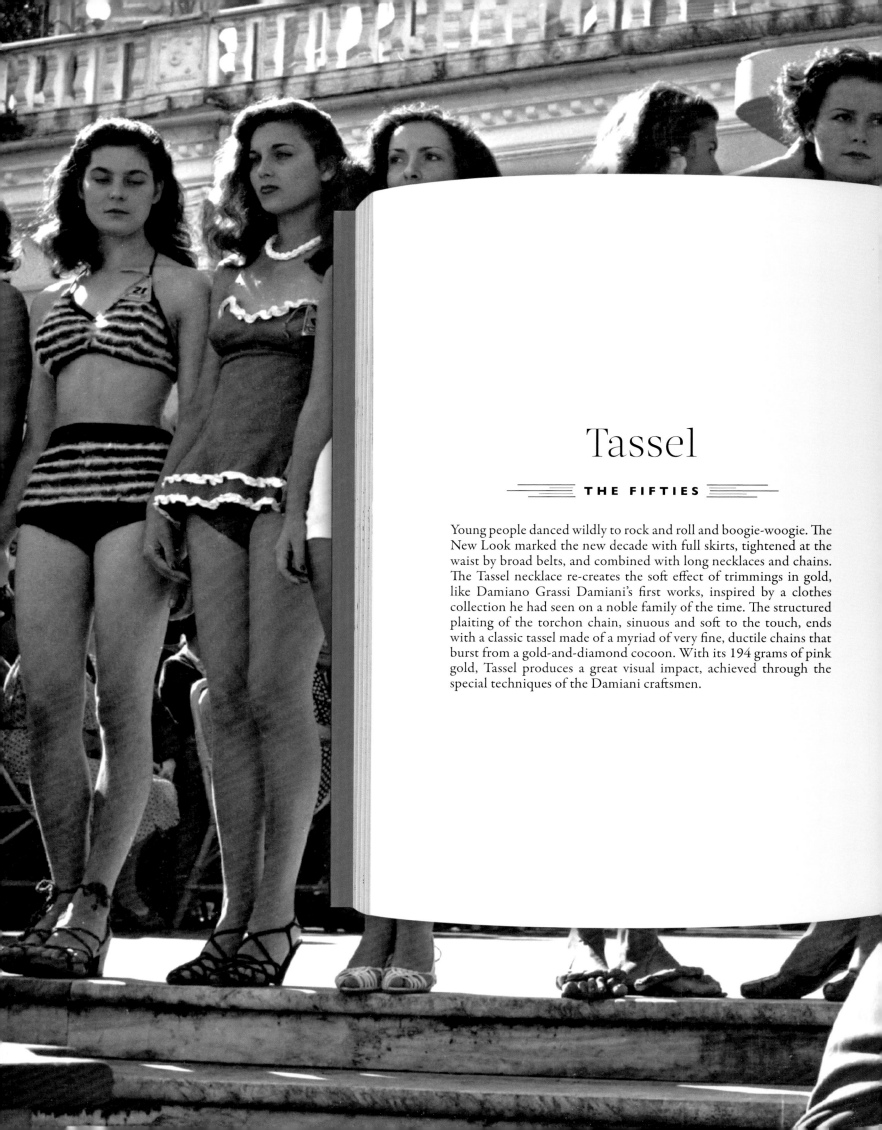

Tassel

Young people danced wildly to rock and roll and boogie-woogie. The New Look marked the new decade with full skirts, tightened at the waist by broad belts, and combined with long necklaces and chains. The Tassel necklace re-creates the soft effect of trimmings in gold, like Damiano Grassi Damiani's first works, inspired by a clothes collection he had seen on a noble family of the time. The structured plaiting of the torchon chain, sinuous and soft to the touch, ends with a classic tassel made of a myriad of very fine, ductile chains that burst from a gold-and-diamond cocoon. With its 194 grams of pink gold, Tassel produces a great visual impact, achieved through the special techniques of the Damiani craftsmen.

MAGIA
FILO RITORTO

CATENE
MOLTO
SOTTILI

Optical

The Optical earrings faithfully express the essence of 1960s style. The greatest challenge in creating these large circles in white gold, enamel, and diamond pavé was to keep the lightness and elegance of the design. The setting of the very luminous pavé on thin sheets of gold is undoubtedly the best expression of Damiani excellence. Mini geometric dresses with black-and-white graphic designs are the ideal counter for this pair of showy pendants, which recall Pop Art, the atmosphere of swinging London, and Damiano's first ideas, when he decided to bring the goldsmiths' art to fashion. Damiano was one of the first jewelers to symbolize jewelry design and make it truly contemporary—while defining his own style.

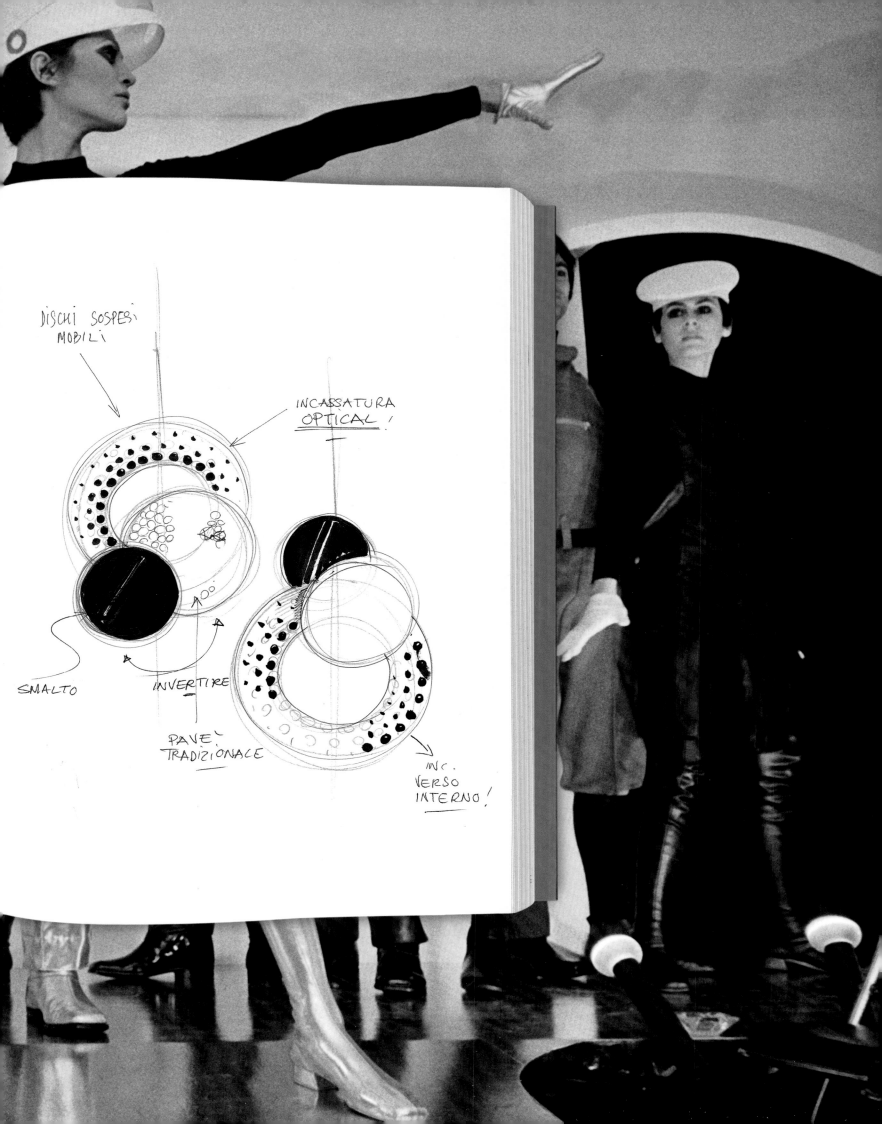

I DON'T EXERCISE. IF GOD HAD WANTED ME TO BEND OVER, HE WOULD HAVE PUT DIAMONDS ON THE FLOOR.

JOAN RIVERS

Bloom

THE SEVENTIES

The 1970s brought another turning point. Young people protested wars and moved toward Eastern religions, and girls decorated their long hair with flowers. Damiano Grassi Damiani drew inspiration from nature, as his children did when they designed Bloom. In this homage to the decade of the flower child, colored stones mingle with 178 white diamonds to create a floral motif. Beautiful flowers to wear round the neck and wrist and also to tie around the forehead like a coronet and whose color combinations required the careful selection of the stones by expert Damiani gemologists.

fiori diversi
"tutti in fila"

Tribute

Tribute represents the hedonistic years that launched logo mania. This imposing domed bracelet spells out the name Damiani. Each letter is formed by one or more gemstones, such as amethysts, citrines, Madera quartz, peridots, prasiolite, and diamonds. The pavé background pays homage to Damiano Grassi Damiani's signature diamond pavé and consists of 1,176 brown, gray, and white diamonds, creating a fantastic, precious mosaic housing splendid, specially hand-cut gemstones—a piece of craftsmanship of great impact, which required many days of work by skilled master setters.

TAGLI E COLORI
diVERSI!!!

DIAMONDS NEVER LEAVE YOU.

SHIRLEY BASSEY

Moonshine

The Moonshine ring pays homage to the 1990s, the years of the pearls that Damiano and his children went all around the world to buy. They were the years that enshrined the advent of new technologies, when the Internet was invaded by images and information. Eight white, gray, and pink pearls were carefully selected for size and color and then set upon a soft pavé of 356 diamonds. Set in bas-relief, they resemble spaceships that are ready for liftoff toward unexplored planets. Moonshine is a metaphor for the desire for new conquests, like those of the international markets that Damiani started to operate in recent years.

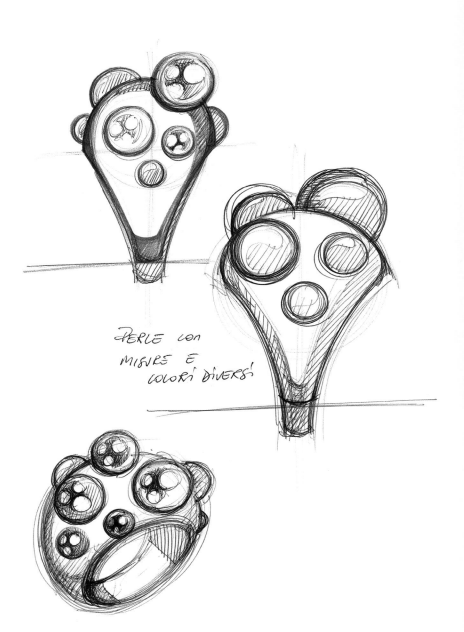

PERLE CON
MISURE E
COLORI DIVERSI

D.Side

This bracelet draws inspiration from D.Side, a collection codesigned with Hollywood star Brad Pitt, which became a symbol of the brand and an icon of the first decade of the twenty-first century. This elegant jewelry is embellished by an exceptional pavé of the whitest of diamonds that embrace the entire circumference in sparkling cross-references, with large brilliant-cut diamonds set in the profile. It took 472 white diamonds, weighing a total of 20 carats, and the careful craftsmanship of master goldsmiths and setters to create it.

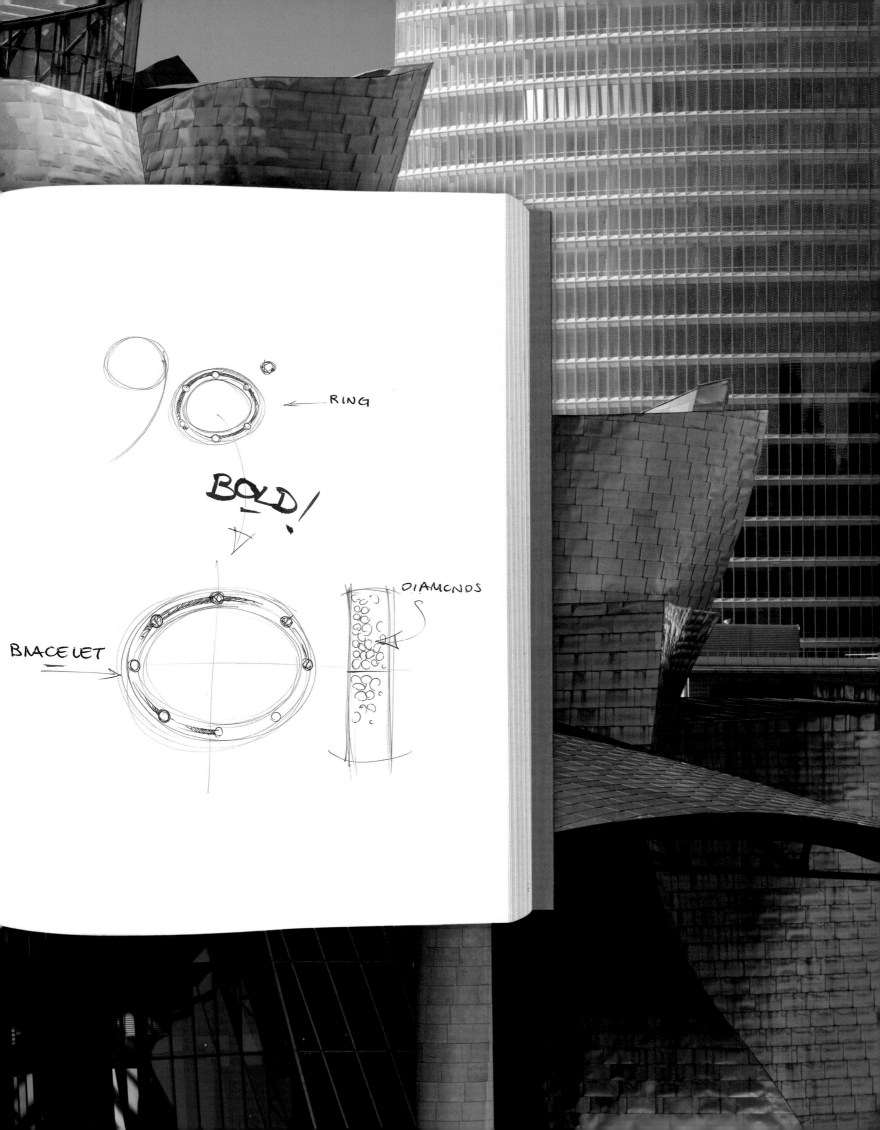

RING

BOLD!

BRACELET

DIAMONDS

DAMIANI
Made in Italy
90th Anniversary
Limited Edition N. 01/09

Damianissima

The succession of *D*s, studded with white diamonds on one side and black ones on the other, make the Damianissima collier a sort of ode to the brand for the 2010s. Throughout its history, Damiani has created unique collections recognizable by its design and making. This pendant is made with 262 white diamonds set into pink gold and the same number of black diamonds set into burnished gold, to give a greater impact to the double-sided effect and the contrasts between black and white.

ELEMENTI
LOGOMANIA
DAMIANISSIMA

A
Family
Story

It's neither the jewel nor the gold nor the diamond,
but something more subtle, unpredictable,
and ephemeral. It's the idea that is most precious.

ENRICO GRASSI DAMIANI

VALENZA, THE CRADLE OF THE ITALIAN GOLDSMITH'S ART

When discussin a successful company like Damiani, with a solid tradition that spans three generations, it's better to start with history and geography. In the shadow of the towers and spires of Italy, various refined skills that make up the origin of the mosaic of knowledge of our country have grown. Even without going back too far in time, it is not far-fetched to say that it was, and still is, the geography of the industrial areas, a configuration unequaled elsewhere, that created and nurtured the miracle of Italian creativity. As Giacomo Becattini writes in his book *Industrial Districts and Made in Italy*, "Right from its very beginning, Italian industry has rested on the small and dispersed. Rather than factories, even if there are plenty of examples through tools and architecture, they are experimental workshops where creative manufacturers work passionately and tenaciously to give shape to visionary ideas [. . .]. Regional roots, family management, i.e. the secrets of making handed down from father to son and the willingness of the new generations, maybe graduates, to treasure the manufacturing experience of their fathers, grafting the shoot of technological innovation onto the old gnarled tree of craftsmanship, form an incomparable pool of skills" (*Distretti industriali e made in Italy*; Bollati Boringhieri; Turin, 1998; p. 85).

Historic Italian companies, created from intuition and courage, have thrived through this type of organization, making the most of regional concentrations. They grew because of their deep-rooted skills and the passion to perform. The geography of the industrial areas matters, but it alone does not explain the creation and growth of the manufacturing companies that became internationally renowned brands.

There is no documented reason for the density of goldsmiths' workshops in Valenza, a town of 20,131 inhabitants in the province of Alessandria, on the right bank of the Po, where 80 percent of the diamonds processed in Italy are set. Perhaps it's purely an accident; a certain tendency toward concentration, probably inherited from the medieval guilds that drove the craftsmen to group their workshops in certain geographical areas.

The father of Valenzan and Italian jewelry is Vincenzo Melchiorre (Valenza, 1845–1925), but the story goes that the first to exercise the craft of goldsmith in his atelier in the Contrada Maestra of Valenza was Francesco Caramora (1797–1827). "His work tools, creations, including elastic bracelets in the form of snakes, coral earrings, and Maltese crosses, were acquired on his premature death by his pupil Pietro Carlo Bartolomeo Conti, who succeeded him in the management of the atelier and goldsmith production. The Conti family was related to the Morosetti and Battaglieri families with whom they also had economic ties. These three families reigned over the jewelers of Valenza with their ateliers specialized in the creating jewelry with a bourgeois taste for more than thirty years" (Lia Lenti, *Valenza ou la joaillerie italienne.* Catalogue of the exhibition of the same name at Petit Palais Beaux Arts, Paris, 8–28 February 2010; Nuvole; 2010; p. 16).

In 1968, the Valenzan creators started to acquire international reputation through the Diamonds International Award and the DeBeers competitions, which started annually in 1954 and were held every two years from 1980 until the last edition in 2000. From 1968 to 1998, the jewelers of Valenza had thirty-three victories, placing them at the top of the Italian classification.

Throughout its history, Damiani has won eighteen Diamonds International Awards, the highest recognition in the world of jewelry, as well as other awards, including two Tahitian Pearl Trophies, a Haute Couture Design Award, and various prizes in the fields of entrepreneurship and communication. As a result, Damiani creations rightfully had the lion's share in the exhibition *Valenza ou la joaillerie italienne* at the Petit Palais in Paris in 2010.

Today Damiani, founded in 1924, is the most important manufacturer that designs, produces, and sells under its own name. In 2011, the city of Valenza dedicated to the company a scenographic fountain and the square in front of the Damiani headquarters, now called Piazza Damiano Grassi Damiani 1.

Maria Grazia Molina, art and jewelry historian and chairperson of Amici del Museo dell'Arte Orafa di Valenza (Friends of the Museum of the Goldsmiths' Art in Valenza) recalls that her uncle Ottavio "learned the craft of goldsmith from Enrico, who everybody considered a precise and patient teacher." She continues, "My father dealt in precious stones and, at the beginning, Damiano bought stones from him. When my father retired and decided not to travel anymore, he passed his list of customers to Damiano with a presentation letter in which he praised his qualities. Damiano was always very grateful for this. He was a very busy businessman, but he always found the time to come and see my father. I still like to remember the appreciation for our organization's goals that Damiano expressed with a substantial donation, at the time of the exhibition 'Oro e Lavoro' (Gold and Work) (1994) and subsequently with the reprinting of our catalogue two years later, thus showing that he had understood the importance and cultural, and promotional, value of the Museo Civico dell'Arte Orafa di Valenza (The Civic Museum of the Goldsmiths' Art in Valenza)."

Valenza, the fountain of Piazza Damiano Grassi Damiani
Opposite: Historic photographs of Valenza

Maria Antonietta Grassi Damiani, Enrico's daughter, recalls, "Like many of his generation, our father was a serious man of few words who never expressed his feelings very much. However, he was always very willing with us children, sometimes almost romantic. I remember that he used to take me out on his bike and tell me stories of places. He also taught me the names of the flowers. Our home, where the Damiani headquarters are still located today, was on the floor above the workshop. That's why I knew everything even though I had never worked in the company. Dad went to work so early that Teresa, our mother, took his breakfast down to him and also did the same for lunch. He worked in a very refined way and everything he designed was harmonious and elegant, like the brooches that were so fashionable at the time and that mum loved so much."

Cover of *L'Orafo valenzano* with Damiani's Albero della Vita
Opposite: Collection of historic advertisements

Damiani

tanti modi   per dire   'amore'

Troverete questi gioielli e molti altri
della collezione *Damiani*
nei migliori negozi italiani

gioielli d' autore

Damiano Grassi Damiani

When I create, I don't think about the jewel but the woman, her tastes and feelings–of that subtle interplay of desires that, in a flash, makes her say "I like it."

DAMIANO GRASSI DAMIANI

THREE SIBLINGS AND A SINGLE GREAT PASSION

It's rare to find a similar harmony and team spirit as that of the Damiani siblings in other family-run companies. The strength of the feeling that unites them is reflected in their words. It's a blood tie, but that's not enough to explain their unusual complicity, their rare harmony in ideas and visions, and their firm conviction in pursuing the same objectives. Perhaps it depends on their devotion to their father, fed by his premature death. Overnight, the Damiani siblings found themselves with a company on their hands. They took on the burden without hesitation, the result of a special apprenticeship and from being close to their father, Damiano, a visionary and decisive man, and his wife, Gabriella, an enterprising and courageous woman, capable of transmitting sincere passion and giving confidence to those around her. The siblings repeatedly mention their father, and he is always part of their tales when speaking about training. Although they attended gemology courses, they attribute their ability to recognize and select gemstones to the example set by their father. They inherited courage, the willingness to take risks, and the prescience of transforming a craftsman trade into a business and giving goldsmith production the added value of a brand with a strong identity from both their father and their mother. It is a project they are successfully developing, expanding in international markets; a result of original, courageous collections that, over time, have defined a unique and identifiable style.

Guido Damiani was born in Alessandria in 1968 and is president and managing director of the Group. He graduated with honors in sociology and holds a degree in gemology. Before entering the family company

Guido Grassi Damiani

in 1994, he worked in the real estate sector, with brilliant results. "I always knew that I would go back to the company," states Guido, "but I wanted to prove to myself that I was able to make out on my own. All three of us felt it was natural to be jewelers. The passion for it was in our blood. We grew up on 'bread and jewelry.' We lived in Valenza. We were 'home and workshop' on the third floor of the building my father constructed, in the same place where our grandfather's workshop was—today, Piazza Damiano Grassi Damiani. In elementary school, once school was over, I went to make paper parcels, typical containers for loose diamonds, earning five lire for each one. I even subcontracted the work to my schoolmates." The story of the paper parcels is an indicator of a precocious managerial vocation, which led to Guido's involvement in marketing and introducing audacious new commercial development strategies. In 1996, he took over the management of the group. The acceleration toward a brand policy, which preserves the original distinctive character of the crafted items and emphasizes the quality of the raw materials and the virtuosity of the processing, is specifically the work of the third generation of the Damiani family. Guido says:

You can't just sit back and wait. You've got to be courageous and fast in decisions.

"And we risked a lot. For example, we opened the first flagship stores, Via Montenapoleone in Milan and Via Condotti in Rome, in one fell swoop. I signed the contracts with my mother, who had the power to sign, when I was twenty-eight, paying millions in goodwill payments. . . . I think it's essential to have your own points of sale. You talk to the consumer through shop windows. My father died suddenly, prematurely, but he'd had the time to pass on the culture of a well-made product, striving toward the best, and the importance of shared work."

Creative Italy is a country of house-factories, and the Damiani Group is no exception, even though it has fifty-nine boutiques around the world and distributes its brands globally. Gabriella, always alongside Damiano Grassi Damiani, in life and at work, still lives in Valenza, in the same place where it all started with Enrico and where, in 2011, a scenographic fountain was inaugurated in memory of her husband. It is a sober building that reveals how the secret of success also depends on the ability to stay loyal to your origins and be rooted in the area. Guido continues, "Working together, ours is organized in choral participation in which each has their tasks. We all cooperate in creation." He then confesses, "Design isn't my specialty, but I also put forward ideas." He has very clear intentions. He knows that to prosper there must be sales, and that you can't just live on awards. Trends in fashion need to be observed carefully, and it is necessary to take account of the context. The Damiani family

Guido Grassi Damiani as a child in the laboratory

Top: The boutiques in Milan and Rome
Middle: The boutique in Milan
Bottom: The boutiques in Shanghai, Moscow, and Singapore

loves innovation and is aware of the importance of fashions. All the collections show a rare balance between innovation and trends. "We were among the first to reintroduce white gold after a long period of obscurity. I believe that the reasons for our success are the strong identity, the great manufacturing ability, and the original design, all encouraged by a great passion. Remember that we started out as designers and producers and that, among the international brands, we are the only ones still owned by the founder's family."

Silvia is the "heart" of the company; vice president of the Damiani Group and responsible for image, she loves to define herself as "the romantic part." She earned a degree in business management and one in gemology at the Istituto Gemmologico Italiano. She loves jewelry so much that she wrote a book, *I gioielli. Istruzioni per l'uso* (*Jewelry: Instructions for Use*; Mondadori; Milan, 1997), where she states in the preface, "The first piece of jewelry I can remember was a diamond and emerald pony. As a child, I went to see it every day and tried it on my dress in a different way each time, looking at the final effect in the mirror. Once the ritual was over, I went home happy. Don't forget, I didn't have to go miles and miles—we lived above the company offices for years. That's why jewelry has always been part of my life. I like jewelry. I like choosing the most beautiful and precious gemstones, imagining the necklaces that will cradle them, studying the pictures for the new collections. And, above all, I like wearing them.

Being an artist isn't enough; you need to be a jeweler.

"This is the simple truth that has guided me in the last few years. When I'm asked if my Grandpa Enrico would have approved of the passage from a small goldsmith's workshop, as his was, to a large company, exactly what Damiani has become today, due to my father's insight, I would say yes, he would have approved because we haven't betrayed his legacy. Each piece of our jewelry is unique; it's manually processed, the gems are rare, and the design is studied in detail."

Silvia is Damiani's ambassador. She has a role similar to that of the itinerant storyteller, the main character in the book of the same name by Mario Vargas Llosa who traveled from village to village, telling

Silvia Grassi Damiani

stories. She tells of her family and how her father, who died at age sixty-one in an accident, passed on the sense of responsibility and dedication to work, how he taught her to recognize gemstones and to trust her intuition, and always encouraged her to get involved with reason and her heart. Silvia continues, "To recount and create, you need to have knowledge. My father was considered a great connoisseur of diamonds; he stirred a sort of reverential awe. The *expertise* in the choice of gemstones can be learned, but, at origin, it's a gift. My father had this gift. When I asked him who he'd learned from, he would say, 'On my own.'

Instead, fate gave us a great master, able to instill confidence. And a great teacher in life, our mother, who is teaching her grandchildren as she taught us.

"I was my father's right hand at just nineteen. He took me to buy gemstones and got me to put them in order of beauty. He considered gems a gift of nature and told me, 'Nature gives us beautiful things; our work is to make them more beautiful.' At twenty-two, he sent me to Japan on my own, aided by three faithful members of staff, to buy pearls. When I traveled, I always carried a note my father had written to me when I was at school, for support: 'It doesn't matter how the exam goes, I really love you.' At first, I even used to phone him at night. He reassured me, 'You've got three things: grit, intuition, and heart, and you must use them in the best way.'"

Giorgio Damiani, born in Alessandria in 1971, is vice president of the Damiani Group. He is the creative director, but doesn't like to be defined as art director. The company is a mission for the brothers and sister, a totality that they take charge of with passion—all together—without hierarchies, subdividing the work naturally. Giorgio says, "We're all creative, even the people making the prototypes; technicians try their hand at creation in their spare time. The collections are created by an internal team of ten designers, five of whom are seniors, who I work with on a daily basis."

We're also able to offer a *tailor-made* service, succeeding in maintaining our identity, consisting of a fluid and highly contemporary design.

Giorgio's words illustrate how many parallels exist between jewelry and couture. The necklaces and bracelets must be soft and supple in order to caress the neck and wrist, and the working on the reverse must be as smooth as velvet. You need to be a jeweler, as Silvia says, but that's not enough to be special. It's worth sharing the secrets of haute couture to create jewelry that dresses with the naturalness of tailored clothing, following the movements of the body. Giorgio continues, "Working on fluid, dynamic lines is difficult. Our model Gomitolo, for example, is incomparable. We created a collection with rough diamonds, the symbol of our connection with Africa, in honor of Sharon Stone. Brad Pitt, for whom we created the engagement ring Promise, came to us because he wanted something very special. We also developed the contemporary and elegant D.Side collection with him. We also create special pieces of jewelry, on request, that aims to satisfy international tastes, too.

Gabriella Grassi Damiani with her children

Giorgio Grassi Damiani

Masterpieces are pieces of jewelry in which we best succeed in expressing our original creativity and the virtuosity of our workmanship.

Beauty also depends on balance and proportions—subtle details that may seem unnecessary but which make the difference in jewelry and work on minimum dimensions. Giorgio underlines the importance of design. His father had already understood that—to be a brand, being excellent craftsmen is not enough, and evolved product development and communication strategies are required, and design must be innovative. While remaining craftsmen, the Damiani family has succeeded in becoming a successful business using product policy and distribution and communication strategies, also the result of an exclusive, modern, sometimes futuristic, design that avoids retro complacency and winks at ethnics while learning from tradition. They have given the added value of the label to jewelry production, promoting appeal and visibility, both with collections with a logo—built around the variations of the initial of the name—and by investing in contemporary design. Materials are very costly at the start, which requires great courage in exposure to risk and awareness of their talent. Giorgio, who is also responsible for the purchase of the gemstones, continues, "We have suppliers all over the world for the purchase of the gems —in Antwerp and Israel for the diamonds; Thailand, Myanmar, and Cambodia for the colored gems; and Colombia for the emeralds."

The Damianis see themselves as craftsmen;
manual skill is at the heart of all the creations
in the workshop in Valenza.

As manufacturers, used to dealing with business, the Damianis cultivate lasting, affectionate relationships with coworkers. Virginio Riboni, who started to work with Enrico Damiani, Damiano's father, at the age of fourteen, has a long memory of the company. At the time, when Damiano was still at school, there were only three young apprentice goldsmiths. "I learned everything from Enrico, a skilled craftsman with great patience," she recalls. "Enrico and his wife were good people and always gave us a bowl of soup at lunchtime. Sometimes Enrico's brother, who lived in Genoa, also came to the workshop. He was a sales representative and also worked at the bench. I remember that one day, while he was cleaning a ring with the brushing machine, the ring flew off and broke the lamp. Being the perfectionist he was, Enrico was angry about the incident and explained to us how the smallest detail should never be ignored. I was only an apprentice, but I heard talk of pieces made for important people, for actresses and ladies of nobility. In 1954, his son Damiano, who was only five years older than me, joined the workshop. Shortly after he entered the company, his father died and Damiano decided to go into dealing in stones. Joined by his wife, Gabriella, he showed those talents for business that led him to lay the foundations of a truly modern company right from the start. He asked me to work for him in the office. I immediately accepted, out of respect for his extraordinary talent, for his friendship, and for the trust I placed in him. We were real friends—during the break, from noon to 2:00 p.m., we played football. In a few years, there were already two hundred of us! The company grew rapidly, but the family spirit wasn't lost. I became the head of the pearl department with twenty-two people reporting to me. I lived near the company, and in the morning took my two daughters to school with Silvia, Guido, and Giorgio. We've always been a family!"

The story of the slender, elegant Lionella Temprini, with fluid speech, still with the company, bears witness to how the Damiani family is perceived by its staff and explains the attraction the company has always had for the people of Valenza, thanks to the brand policy with its own stylistic hallmark and its ability to conquer the international markets—an open window on the world, which enabled horizons to be extended beyond a provincial life. Lionella comes from Rovigo, in northeast Italy. She studied to become a teacher and taught in elementary school for eight years. She says, "I've always kept myself busy. I worked in after-school activities and school lunches and, at nineteen, I taught the immigrants from the south of Italy to read and write. To supplement my income, I also did the cards [the technical indications on the piece of jewelry, i.e., the reference, the weight of gold, carats of the gems and price, handwritten with the rapidograph] for Damiani. December 27, 1969, was my first working day for Damiani doing the cards. The company was growing; it had started doing fairs and offered to employ me. I had to decide—continue being an elementaryschool teacher or be taken on by Damiani. I chose the company." She continues, "At the beginning, the three siblings were still children and sat beside Gabriella, their mother. I loved them as if they were my own.

The Damianis have jewelry in their blood, and they're innovators, whether in design, in the use of the gems, and marketing.

"Damiano Grassi Damiani invested in new things and knew how to expose them in an original way. In the company, nothing escaped him. He dealt with everything, from the furnishing, the stands, to the cases for the jewelry. At fairs, Damiani was the first to have a kitchen in the stand and to use open showcases in order to get the company to be known and appreciated by visitors." She strings together one memory after another, and her eyes shine because she also thinks of Damiani as something of her own and feels privileged to be part of it. She could be considered as one of the family because of the emotion she shows by her memories and the precision with which she lists the iconic products of the company, putting them in precise chronological order, like the pearls of a necklace.

Luciana Zunino joined the company in October 1967 as Damiano Grassi Damiani's secretary. She then moved to the pearl department, where she still works. "When I started working for the company," she remembers, "Silvia Damiani was one year old and there were just a few of us—it was like a family. That's why I was so moved when the company was listed on the Stock Exchange in 2007.
"Working alongside Damiano was great schooling for me. I learned a lot, most of all precision and passion for the work. That's what makes the difference. I remember when I was asked to choose the pearls, a gesture of great trust by the owner. I chose them and Mr. Damiani approved the selection, asking me to make the point for the pin. When he gave them back, they were all fine except for one, where Mr. Damiani's point covered half of mine. He was right!" The anecdote shows the attention that Damiano had for every detail and the sharpness of his eye, which missed nothing. He had good sight but was attentive to every detail, realizing the value of a brand before the others. He always talked of opening single brand shops when it seemed like madness. He left us a seed—the passion for a job done well, the only thing that he understood.
"He gave confidence to his staff and never opposed them, always showing great respect for the work of others. He was also a good-looking man, who worked hard, but also liked to enjoy himself." She adds, "I remember that once, in Japan, some girls thought he was Gregory Peck and he, unperturbed, gave them autographs. He loved songs and singing. Sometimes," she concludes flirtatiously, "he asked me to sing the songs that were running through his head."

Rosy Fico, who has been with the company for more than forty years, also started working for Damiani making the papers. "I learned from the older girls," she says. "There's always been a feeling of belonging in the company, almost as though we were all part of a large family. I later worked alongside Gabriella; I helped her to prepare the goods for the fairs and meetings. Then I managed the credit office for about twenty years, until 2000, and then I worked in sales until 2006. Subsequently I moved to sales organization, and today I'm the area manager north and trade marketing." She remembers Damiano, his severity, and humanity, and her eyes fill with tears. She recalls, "In the morning, he may have reprimanded you, but the same evening, he would ask you about your family. He looked for every shaft of natural light to assess the stones, even under the desk! He even taught me how to shake hands. You must transmit warmth, he repeated. At fairs, we all went to dinner together and then, at the end of the meal, we all sang in chorus and Mr. Damiani could be heard because of the warm note of his voice."

Giorgio Vrello, who has worked in administration since 1974, recalls, "At the time, the workshop was much smaller than it is today, and we couldn't meet the many orders. We gave work to five hundred chosen craftsmen in the area. Mr. Damiani was severe and expected a great deal from his staff, also because he never spared himself. But he was a fair person, with great charisma, able to convince and stimulate. A visionary who, already in 1979, decided to move the company offices to a period building in the center of Milan, although the heart of the production was in Valenza. I learned from him the determination to pursue my aims and obtain results."

Giorgio Andreone, lecturer in jewelry design at the Istituto Statale d'Arte, Valenza, and founder of the Orafo valenzano, the official magazine of the local goldsmiths' association, which periodically documents what is happening in Valenzan jewelry, entered the sphere of Damiani in the 1970s. His meeting with Damiano Grassi Damiani was a sort of thunderbolt. "Damiano was a man of quick, sudden decisions. He immediately asked me to create a brochure for the company. The day his son, Giorgio, was baptized, he came to my home to ask me to join the company. I accepted, but I continued teaching. Apart from lessons, I spent all my time at the Damiani workshop from March 1971 until my retirement in 1989. When I joined the company, there weren't many people in the offices in Valenza; a few years later there were more than two hundred. Damiano wanted me to review everything and to improve the operation of the company. We were always a large family, and I'm not only talking about the family metaphorically; there are generations of relatives in the company."

Damiano was impulsive, quick to make decisions on which he rarely went back; he had formidable insight—he never made mistakes about people. A special admiration for Damiano can be felt in Giorgio Andreone's emotional story, although he acknowledges the harsh aspects of Damiano's character. "He was a charming man, a special mix, an impetuous and determined man but loyal, able to make himself be loved, also because his way of being demanding stimulated everyone, he himself was the first to do his best."

There's another longtime coworker alongside Giorgio, for the acquisition of gemstones—Albarosa Vescovo. She joined the company in 1976, where her father and brother already worked, after starting the craft in another company at the age of fifteen. She gained experience alongside Damiano Grassi Damiani. "I never attended any professional school and I don't have a degree in gemology," she says with undisguised pride. "I started looking at the gems with Mr. Damiani. He classified them and I watched. I learned from his looks." She continues, "A special sensitivity, generally more feminine than masculine, is required for the colored gems. The sensitivity refines when you assess many gems on a daily basis, but, most of all, you must like them. For many coworkers, the training consisted of Damiano's example. They learned from his intuition and courage to innovate. In this way, they learned to classify the gems by looking at them repeatedly and not according to the rules, sharpening the eye in continuous observance, treasuring the secrets of a skill acquired in the field." She resumes, "Gemologists know the basics, but don't have the experience. Each gem is a new discovery. And each time you marvel the wonders nature is capable of. Today, this work is simpler because all the gemstones are certificated, starting from 0.3 carats, whereas before there were only the larger ones. Gemstones are examined with a lens that magnifies by ten, immersed in alcohol; even a speck of dust can be taken for an inclusion. For colored ones, master stones act as a parameter. In Antwerp, they bring you parcel paper as big as a wallet, even of 1,000 grams (5 carats make a gram). It's always a marathon there; previews of hundreds of gems are made in a very short space of time. Those chosen are sent to the workshop for the final selection. The purchase of gemstones has very old rules, based on trust."

Every deal is closed with a handshake, saying the word *mazal*, when there is a consolidated relationship with the suppliers. This also applies to telephone deals.

She concludes, "When I select gems, it's as though I'm buying them for myself. I feel as though I'm partly the creator of each piece of jewelry and I'm proud to be able to say this to the customers. I feel like the member of a family who has been able to transmit the conviction that I'm part of its success. Passion and gratification are the keys to my loyalty to the Damiani brand." Albarosa identifies herself with the company so much that she often speaks in the plural form. Once again, it's a special kind of devotion.

Sante Rizzetto, a famed setter, has been doing his job for more than fifty years, and boasts of being able to instantly recognize his setting. "Each goldsmith has his or her own method. There's a personal way of pulling the prongs and making the base. Each setter has his own identifiable style, but before that, there are the companies. Damiani, for example, has decided that the gemstone must fit well into the basketlike base. I make sure I'm recognized, because I fit it a little bit higher," concludes Sante. He was willing to be put to the test, and he instantly found those he had set from a number of rings with 0.30 diamonds. It seems impossible that Sante's large hands are able to handle diamonds of 0.30 carats with just the help of pincers, and that his eyes are able to recognize even the smallest stones without a microscope. "It's a question of practice," he asserts. "Eyes can be trained to look and hands to handle." He concludes, "My hands have only shaken once—when I met Sharon Stone, who came to visit the workshop in Valenza."

It's rare to hear so much sincere participation in the destiny of the company and so much spontaneous involvement in the production of the articles in the words of the staff. In Valenza, everybody knows one another and stays together, but habit can't be the only explanation for the attachment to work, something expressed by many people who have worked and still work for this company.

Creativity and skill in execution don't explain the admiration, devotion, and loyalty shown by all employees and coworkers; it's almost as if Damiani is also a family affair for them. This admiration and devotion are evident in a letter in memory of Damiano Grassi Damiani written by all his employees upon his death: "Belonging to Damiani means being part of a great project, a great dream of a man who dedicated his life, energy, love, and unwavering passion to his work and his company. This is why, on the death of Mr. Damiani, we're not only mourning the owner but the man. Our hearts, our affections, and our tears are for him, but they also speak to Gabriella, his wife and loyal partner, and Silvia, Guido, and Giorgio, the children who he had already called to work by his side for some time. We want to say to them that we are with you in the important task that awaits you."

Each
Creation,
an
Image

I become fond, I always like to have a family and, when I go to Milan, Damiani is my family and I like that very much. There's a lot of warmth and esteem.

SOPHIA LOREN

YESTERDAY, TODAY, AND DAMIANI

I've seen Sophia Loren in action in front of a foreign audience at least a couple of times. The first was at the Academy offices in Los Angeles in the spring of 2012. It was an evening in her honor to celebrate the fiftieth anniversary of the first of her two Oscars, the one she won for the interpretation of Vittorio De Sica's *Ciociara*. Presented onstage by Billy Crystal and later celebrated at dinner by Warren Beatty, Al Pacino, and John Travolta, Loren, speaking English without hesitation, enchanted all the disenchanted Hollywood stars. She wore a diamond choker around her neck and a pair of long sparkling earrings, dream jewelry branded Damiani, but, in the meantime, she told rather earthly anecdotes, such as "that time when Carlo Ponti, my husband, told me off because I used the knife to cut an omelet. I've never ordered an omelet in a restaurant since then."

As if there was any need for it, I had the second proof of Sophia Loren's very special charisma, made of unattainable myth and warmth at the same time, on a very different occasion. It was in November 2012, during a press conference with Giorgio Damiani, for an event with the company's customers. We were in a hotel overlooking the sea at Noordwijk aan Zee, thirty minutes from Amsterdam. It was a bitterly cold, windy day, but Loren immediately warmed the atmosphere with the most economic and renewable energy of all—her friendliness. She and Giorgio transformed the meeting into a lively three-way conversation between the actress, businessman, and the public. A Dutch journalist asked her if she preferred to be called Mrs. Loren or Mrs. Ponti, and she answered promptly and in a ringing tone, "Sophia!"

Sophia, that's all. As Silvia Damiani says, "The more you get to know her, the more fond of her you become." The link between the actress and the family of jewelers is lost in the mists of time. "Today, Sophia, who is the same age as our mother who, in turn, adores her just as our father adored her, is part of our family history," says Silvia. "Among ourselves, we say that my brother Giorgio must have confided in her personal things that we have never known and will never know."

When asked, Giorgio Damiani neither confirms nor denies it. But in a sly voice he says, "She's our patron and, on the other hand, we're a family company, not a brand run by managers who are here today, and tomorrow are working somewhere else. The relationship with Sophia and her family has grown naturally, over time. And then we're down-to-earth people with our feet on the ground, just like her, as becoming a star hasn't changed her clear, straightforward character one bit."

Guido says, "One thing is certain, Sophia Loren is much more than an endorser for Damiani—she's an ambassador."

Until a few years ago, jewelry was advertised in one way: with still-life photographs of the products. There were no models, much less actresses, wearing necklaces and earrings in the pages of magazines or catalogs; only on red carpets. Silvia recalls, "My father personally followed the work of the photographers. He was obsessed with the search for the perfect light that best enhanced the precise work and the brightness of the gold and gemstones. Then, in the 1980s, we did our first press campaign with a spokesperson, and it opened a new road."

The turning point was no accident. At that time, market research indicated that jewelry photographed on its own gave the consumer the optical illusion of being four or five times larger than it really was and, therefore, more expensive. Displaying it on a person restored the proportions more precisely and encouraged the temptation to buy. One of the first stars of the Damiani campaign was Isabella Rossellini. The idea came to Silvia during one of many business trips to China. "I was at the border between China and Hong Kong, which was still a British colony at the time, waiting for the visa. There was a very small duty-free shop full of obsolete Chinese objects, but the area for cosmetics was well stocked. There was an enormous poster with the face of Isabella Rossellini, the testimonial for a cream, on one wall; a beautiful woman with international appeal and yet profoundly Italian. In that instant, I decided that I would convince my father to do a campaign with her."

And that's what happened. Isabella Rossellini was the face of the Damiani campaigns for four years—the first step toward an increasingly varied way of communication, of which Sophia Loren has been an integral part for many years. The actress represents the Damiani brand around the world and takes part in the company's most important events. She often travels with Giorgio, who remembers their first journey together: "We were at the airport, going from Los Angeles to New York. Everybody imaginable was there, from teenagers to old people, and they greeted her in every possible language saying, 'You're very beautiful, you're fantastic.' Together, we went to those new worlds for the market, like China. Even there, she's an icon of style and femininity. For me, every trip with her is also an example of extraordinary discipline and professionalism—never late, never a moment of distraction. She's simply impeccable and if, for some reason, we're imprecise, she yells. Rightfully so."

Sophia Loren also wears Damiani jewelry in all her public appearances, like the Academy Awards and similar events. Silvia says, "I particularly remember an evening at the Scala, in Milan, many years ago. She was dressed in Armani and was wearing the Vulcania necklace, one of our Masterpieces, in three colors with fancy, brown, and white

diamonds. Giorgio Armani, who accompanied her and doesn't usually like bejeweled women because momentous jewelry is not always in tune with certain dresses, said to her, 'You're perfect,' and she replied, 'I feel exactly like a queen because instead of having a crown on my head, it's round my neck.' It was one of the times that fashion fans call a 'historical fashion moment'— King Giorgio Armani with Queen Sophia Loren at his side."

However, the association with Damiani is not limited to these occasions. Sophia Loren has collaborated for many years in the creation of a range that bears her name. As she said in an interview for *Prestige* magazine in Singapore, "At the beginning, when I met the Damianis, we started to talk about jewelry, how it's made and where the stones and diamonds are found. They saw that I was interested in the choice of colors and designs. They liked my ideas, and slowly but surely, we became friends. They showed me some sketches to get my opinion, and then they thought that I could give them some ideas. It was something very spontaneous."

Silvia adds, "The Sophia Loren collection is one of the first collections in which we used pink gold. She liked it, and it was in tune with the elegance of the 1950s, which she represents so well."

Every piece labeled Loren is a great success. As Guido says, "The fact that she wears a piece of jewelry, or even labels it, doubles the dream that we sell. It's closer to the myth." An enduring myth, one with the idea of Italy as the cradle of elegance and creativity, but also hard work and the sense of family—values that the Damiani family has always represented. "We're very proud to be Italian, more so today, now that we're a rarity—a completely Italian brand for ninety years," says Guido. "Having Sophia as the symbol is an accolade that honors us. I appreciate her very much also because, beyond her great talent as an actress and her international fame, she always stresses the hard times of her childhood. She inspires positivity, she's a model of will and perseverance. Meeting her and spending time with her, as it turned out for our family, has been very lucky for us. Because she's a myth that never disappoints."

edited by
PAOLA JACOBBI

I tell the Damianis to go on, to believe in what they do and they've shown it . . . we go around the world and we open five, six, ten boutiques, which means that they're very successful. I'm very proud of them.

SOPHIA LOREN

The Damianis have always been innovators, not just in the collections but also in communication, starting with Damiano, who united a conscious entrepreneurial vision with precise awareness of what it means to be brand.

CREATIONS SPEAK FOR THEMSELVES

Silvia says that her father already entrusted advertising campaigns to talented photographers who were able to capture the reflections of the gems. Each year, a photo shoot with a precise setting was commissioned to present the new creations.

Originating from the research of De Beers, which showed that still-life shots were not able to convey the perception of the magic given by jewelry when it was worn, Silvia convinced her father to return to shooting jewelry worn by models after several campaigns using still life.

This was the third generation's real achievement—leading the world of jewelry out of a static tradition toward a dynamic, versatile, and daily dimension by implementing a strategic change in company communications. Damiani adopted the use of international spokespeople creating a prestigious gallery of portraits that includes, among others, Isabella Rossellini, photographed by Dominique Isserman, Miles Aldridge, and Fabrizio Ferri; Brad Pitt, the first male spokesperson, who also labeled the D.Side collection, photographed by Peter Lindbergh; Chiara Mastroianni, Milla Jovovich, Nastassja Kinski, and Jennifer Aniston also photographed by Lindbergh; then, Gwyneth Paltrow photographed by Sante D'Orazio; and Sharon Stone, photographed by Sølve Sundsbø.

The 2012–2013 campaign, created under the supervision of Silvia Grassi Damiani and the artistic direction of Paul Barry, with shots by Richard Foster for still life and by Greg Williams for worn jewelry, inaugurated a new hybrid formula uniting worn jewelry with still life. A Polaroid is placed on every photo, almost casually, that sharply presents the jewelry almost in 3-D. The pictures combine the emotional and descriptive story, giving a dual reading that makes you dream about and gain familiarity with the product.

It's a story with a certain irony and sense of humor, something that doesn't usually happen in jewelry advertising; it plays with male-female ambiguity. I go into the drawing room, take off my coat, and move toward an outline of a shadow that appears to be that of a male, but, in reality, it's only me. Damiani's message not only reinforces the concept that a woman can buy herself jewelry but also conveys this idea of ambiguity that could be the symbol of this end of millennium.

ISABELLA ROSSELLINI
Vogue Spain, July 25, 1999

Previous pages: Isabella Rossellini, photographed by Dominique Issermann
Isabella Rossellini, photographed by Fabrizio Ferri

GWYNETH PALTROW, 77th Academy Awards, Los Angeles, 2005
DITA VON TEESE, 66th Cannes Festival, 2013
LIVIA GIUGGIOLI and **COLIN FIRTH**, Golden Globes, Beverly Hills, 2012
LI BINGBING, 64th Cannes Festival, 2011
LUISA RANIERI, Montecarlo Film Festival, 2013
GIANNA JUN, 64th Cannes Festival, 2011
GUIDO DAMIANI and **YOSHINO KIMURA**, 2013
GIORGIO DAMIANI, JOAQUÍN CORTÉS, and **GUIDO DAMIANI**, 2003
GUIDO DAMIANI and **LILIAN THURAM**, 2005
LI BINGBING, 64th Cannes Festival, 2011
SILVIA DAMIANI and **PATRICK DEMPSEY**, 2008
GIORGIO DAMIANI and **ORNELLA MUTI**, Rome, 2003
SILVIA DAMIANI and **SARAH FERGUSON**, Milan, 2001

ALIYA NAZARBAYEVA, 2011
PENÉLOPE CRUZ, Milan, 2004
GIORGIO DAMIANI and HELEN MIRREN, 2009
SILVIA DAMIANI and LAURA PAUSINI, Milan, 2002
MILLA JOVOVICH, 66th Cannes Festival, 2013
ANDY YAN, GIANNA JUN, LI BINGBING, WENDI DENG MURDOCH,
GIORGIO DAMIANI, and FLORENCE SLOAN,
64th Cannes Festival, 2011
ANDIE MACDOWELL and her daughter
SARAH MARGARET QUALLEY,
65th Cannes Festival, 2012
ZHANG ZIYI, 2013
GUIDO DAMIANI with Juventus in Japan, 2005
SILVIA DAMIANI, ISABELLA ROSSELLINI,
and CAROLINE DI MONACO, 2004
GUIDO DAMIANI and SOFIA MILOS, 2006

Brad Pitt, advertising campaign 2000, photographed by Peter Lindbergh

I'm happy to have worked with Damiani to produce
the D.Side range of jewelry together.
If it were up to me, I'd never give up this kind
of relationship. I love it.

BRAD PITT
May 17, 2004

Nastassja Kinski, advertising campaign 2001, photographed by Peter Lindbergh
Opposite: Chiara Mastroianni, advertising campaign 2001, photographed by Peter Lindbergh

ANELLI FOREVER E ORECCHINI TORCHON • CHIARA MASTROIANNI FOTOGRAFATA DA PETER LINDBERGH.

TILDA SWINTON, 80th Academy Awards, Los Angeles, 2008
SHARON STONE, Milan, 2012
CATHERINE DENEUVE, Rome, 2004
AL PACINO and SILVIA DAMIANI, Rome Film Festival, 2008
CLINT EASTWOOD and SILVIA DAMIANI, Los Angeles, 2007
CLAUDIA CARDINALE, 2004
TILDA SWINTON and SILVIA DAMIANI, Milan, 2009
GUIDO DAMIANI, GEENA DAVIS, and SILVIA DAMIANI, 2006

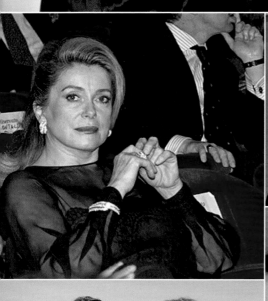

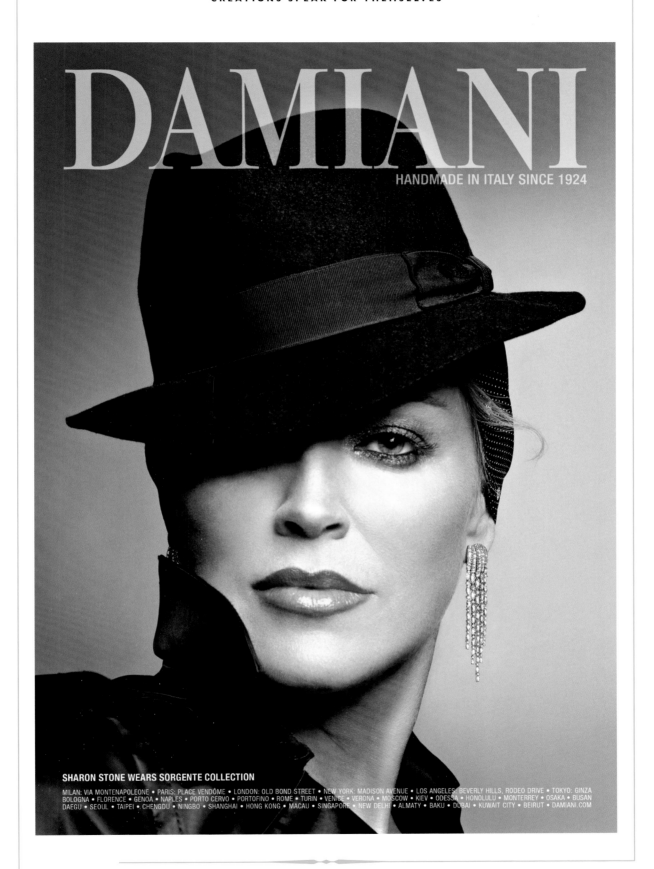

Sharon Stone, advertising campaign 2008, photographed by Sølve Sundsbø

COLLEZIONE EDEN • JENNIFER ANISTON FOTOGRAFATA DA PETER LINDBERGH.

NELLE BOUTIQUES DAMIANI - MILANO: VIA MONTENAPOLEONE, 10 • ROMA: VIA CONDOTTI, 84 • FIRENZE: VIA DE' TORNABUONI, 30/32R • VENEZIA: SALIZADA S.MOISE'/SAN MARCO, 1494 • BARI: VIA SPARANO, 52 • NAPOLI: VIA CALABRITTO, 5 • PORTOCERVO: PIAZZETTA PORTOCERVO • PORTOFINO: CALATA MARCONI, 3 • TORINO: VIA LAGRANGE, 40 • VERONA: VIA MAZZINI, 59 • PARIS: PLACE VENDOME, 2 • MADRID: CALLE JOSÈ ORTEGA Y GASSET, 16 • BERLIN: FASANENSTRASSE, 22 • MOSCOW • KIEV • DUBAI • TOKYO • OSAKA • FUKUOKA • HONG KONG • SEOUL • BUSAN • HONOLULU - E NELLE MIGLIORI GIOIELLERIE. PER INFORMAZIONI: 800-56.56.56 - WWW.DAMIANI.IT

DAMIANI

Jennifer Aniston, advertising campaign 2002, photographed by Peter Lindbergh

GUIDO DAMIANI and VIKTOR VEKSEL'BERG, Moscow, 2013
PARIS HILTON and GUIDO DAMIANI, Tokyo, 2009
KASIA SMUTNIAK, 65th Cannes Festival, 2012
EVA LONGORIA, 65th Cannes Festival, 2012
GERALDINE CHAPLIN, Los Angeles, 2003
CRISTIANA CAPOTONDI, 68th Venice Film Festival, 2011

Milla Jovovich, advertising campaign 2001, photographed by Peter Lindbergh

Gwyneth Paltrow, advertising campaign 2006, photographed by Sante D'Orazio

GUIDO DAMIANI, ANG LEE, and SILVIA DAMIANI
GIANNA NANNINI, LAPO ELKANN, and SILVIA DAMIANI,
Milan, 2008
GUIDO DAMIANI, SILVIA DAMIANI, and PETER LINDBERGH,
Milan, 2002
GUIDO DAMIANI and LUCIANO PAVAROTTI, 2004
RICHARD GERE, CAREY LOWELL, and SILVIA DAMIANI, 2004
QIN HAILU, Milan, 2012
GUIDO DAMIANI, SHARON STONE, and GIORGIO DAMIANI,
Milan, 2012
GIORGIO DAMIANI, BRAD PITT, and GUIDO DAMIANI,
Tokyo, 2004
MADALINA GHENEA, Roma, 2013
GWYNETH PALTROW, Tokyo, 2005
RON HOWARD, SILVIA DAMIANI, and TOM HANKS, Roma, 2008
GIORGIO DAMIANI, SHARON STONE, and SILVIA DAMIANI,
62nd Cannes Festival, 2009
GUIDO DAMIANI and ERIC BANA, Tokyo, 2004
SHARON STONE and GIORGIO DAMIANI
SILVIA DAMIANI, GWYNETH PALTROW,
and GIORGIO DAMIANI, Los Angeles, 2007
EMANUELE FILIBERTO DI SAVOIA and SILVIA DAMIANI,
Milan, 2006

I've been collaborating with Damiani for years, and I wear their beautiful jewelry. For a woman, wearing jewelry is the most attractive thing there is. It can never be considered a job.

SHARON STONE

We've been able to offer wells with drinking water to African villages and schools because of Damiani and a range of jewelry called Maji.

SHARON STONE

A GIFT TO GIVE BACK

The Damianis are aware that they are indebted to nature. They learned this from their father, who loved repeating, "Nature gives us beautiful things; our work is to make them even more beautiful."

Diamonds mostly come from Africa, and they are the wealth of a continent where living conditions are critical, mainly because of the chronic lack of drinking water, something far more precious than gems, and upon which the survival of so many populations depends. So the Damiani family decided to start an international project to support African populations, committing themselves directly to offering practical help to the people living near the diamond mines. They designed a collection called Maji, which means "water" in Swahili, with American actress Sharon Stone, who has always been responsive to social causes and who is especially sensitive to the difficulties of the weak. Part of the profits from the sale of pieces in the Maji collection were donated to Drop in the Bucket, a nongovernment and nonprofit humanitarian association that is committed to bringing drinking water to the remotest African villages, contributing to the reduction of a very high mortality rate, particularly infant mortality. In 2009, Giorgio Damiani traveled in sub-Saharan Africa with Sharon Stone to see this dramatic situation firsthand and to share the project with Desmond Tutu and the late Nelson Mandela.

The Maji collection is dedicated to Africa also in the aesthetics. The materials used—which include burnished silver and sanded yellow gold, combined with rough diamonds, each different from one another and all unique in their imperfection, deliberately mounted irregularly—have a "wild" look to them

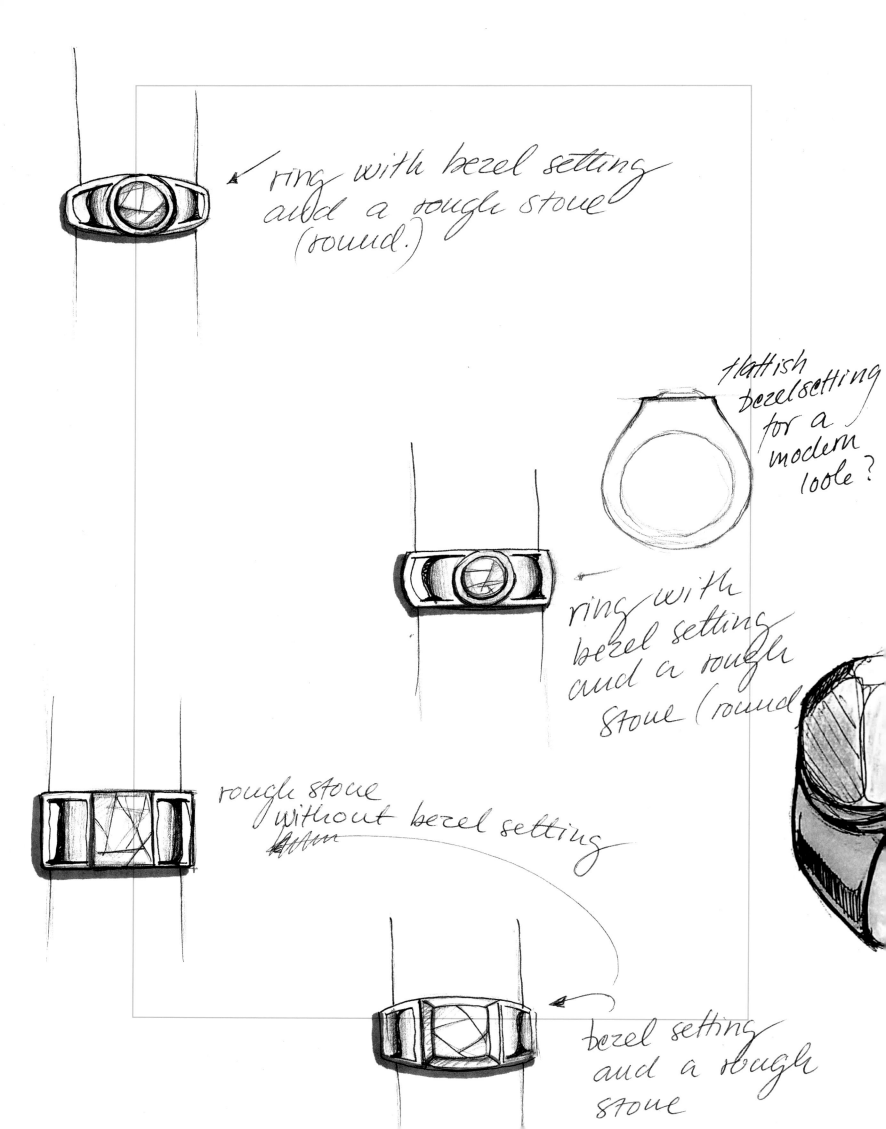

ring with bezel setting
and a rough stone
(round.)

flattish
bezel setting
for a
modern
look?

ring with
bezel setting
and a rough
stone (round.

rough stone
without bezel setting

bezel setting
and a rough
stone

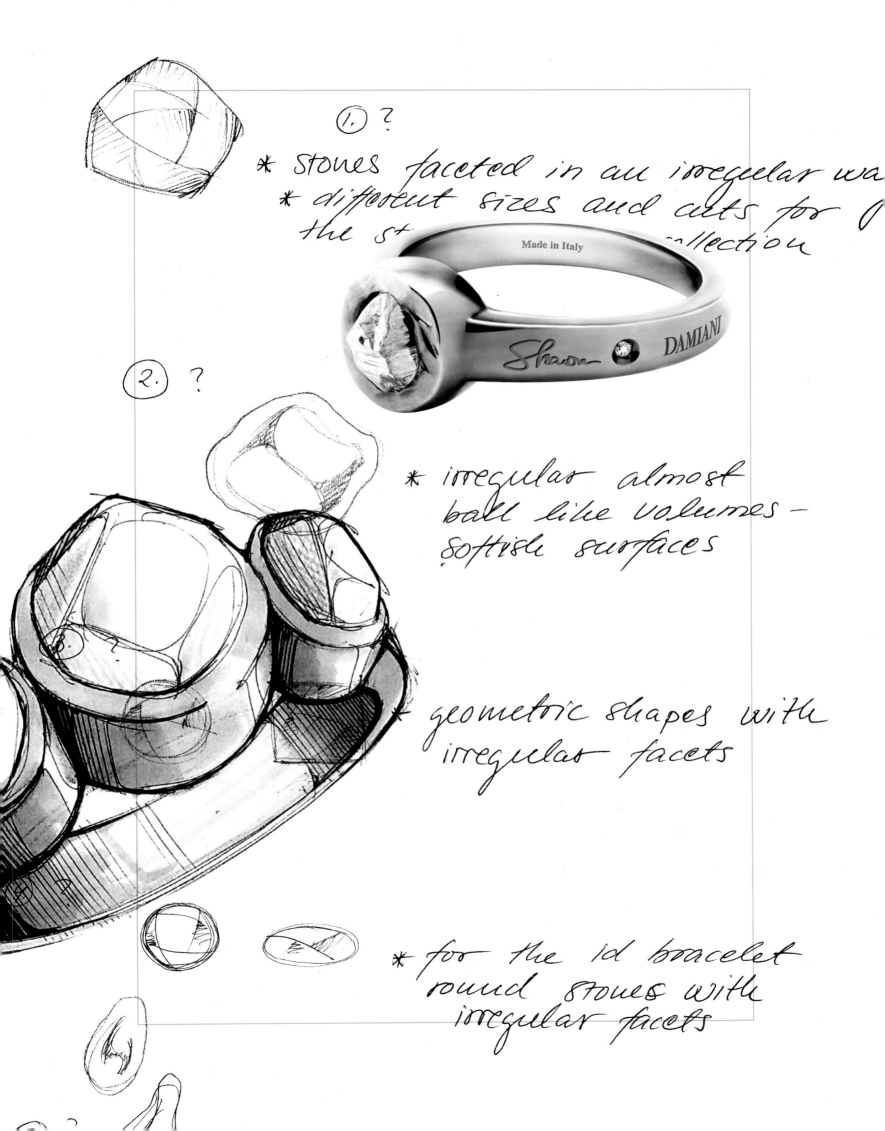

① ?

* stones faceted in an irregular wa...
* different sizes and cuts for ...
  the st... ...llection

② ?

* irregular almost
  ball like volumes -
  softish surfaces

* geometric shapes with
  irregular facets

* for the id bracelet
  round stones with
  irregular facets

Made in Italy

Sharon   DAMIANI

Top: Sharon Stone and Giorgio Damiani at the inauguration of a well, 2009
Middle left: Sharon Stone, Archbishop Desmond Tutu, and Giorgio Damiani **Middle right:** Giorgio Damiani and Nelson Mandela
Bottom: Children expressing thanks

and reflect African atmospheres. Each piece in this special series bears Sharon's engraved signature and the Damiani brand.

The launch of the Maji project, with Sharon Stone as the ambassador, took place in Tokyo in November 2009. A year later, in December 2010, during an event at the Beverly Wilshire Hotel in Los Angeles, Sharon Stone, Silvia Damiani, and John Travis, chairman of Drop in the Bucket, celebrated the first results of the project, which had enabled the construction of fifty new wells in Africa, supplying drinking water to more than ten thousand people. The project continues to this day with the opening of new wells.

The charity work in Africa is not only an important humanitarian commitment of the Damiani Group, but, in its own right, belongs to the brand's work of design and development, strengthening the company's link with the land of origin of the precious materials that nurture its virtuous work. It is a gift in return that increases the iconic value of the collections. An ethical company by strategy and management, starting from the rigorous choices of the gemstones, all supplied with a conflict-free certificate, Damiani has chosen to be transparent, aware that it can't remain unresponsive to what is happening in the world.

Sharon Stone and Giorgio Damiani during their trip to Africa in 2009

From Stones *to* Jewelry

This jewel already existed, among the things of always, among the thousand shapes that, like a cocoon, enclose the creations. A world of signs that speak to us every day. The secret of creativity is to know how to listen to it.

DAMIANO GRASSI DAMIANI

DIAMONDS ARE A GIRL'S BEST FRIEND

"*Diamonds are a girl's best friend*," sang Marilyn Monroe, embodying the desire for luxury that was led by the upturn after the Second World War. Diamonds, famous for their rarity, perfection, and light, continue to sparkle among human desires. As Zsa Zsa Gábor once said, "I never hated a man enough to give him his diamonds back." The symbol of wealth and strength, diamonds' immortality has fascinated generations of beautiful women, the likes of Sophia Loren, Isabella Rossellini, Jennifer Aniston, Gwyneth Paltrow, and Sharon Stone—sensuous, brilliant women who have been able to interpret vanity and luxury and, implicitly, wealth; the inseparable reason of the most beautiful Damiani jewelry.

The diamond—a fragment of heaven and eternity, from the Greek *adamas*, meaning hardest metal— holds exceptional hardness at 10 Mohs (the maximum value on the Mohs scale of mineral hardness), notable tenacity in terms of impact absorption and heat resistance; features that, through the centuries, have made the diamond the emblem of power and the privilege of few.

The diamond's journey, both in nature and history, to be crowned king of the precious stones is a long one. Fire and stone melted together into a single form, an indestructible stone par excellence, a concentration of infinite powers; considered the third eye, the revealer of the soul of the wearer, and set into rings and mounted on objects of worship or crowns of the whole world, fascinating and nurturing the idea of a divine power.

There are many court portraits showing clothes and jewelry belonging to kings and queens of different ages where diamonds embody the assertion of power. The very beautiful, anonymous portrait of Catherine de' Medici, Queen of France in the middle of the sixteenth century, is displayed in the Galleria degli Uffizi. Equally magnificent is the work of Frans Pourbus, who portrays Maria de' Medici in a coronation dress, with the famous Beau Sancy diamond of 34.98 carats set into the crown, which was subsequently passed from generation to generation of European royal families and then sold in Geneva in May 2012; and the portrait of Queen Marie Leszczyńska, bride of Louis XV of France, painted by Charles-André Vanloo, with the pendant Sancy diamond of 55.23 carats, a gift from Cardinal Mazarin. There are many other paintings in which we can admire emperors and empresses, like Catherine II of Russia, portrayed in imperial clothes by Vigilius Eriksen, wearing the crown of Russia, created in 1762 with 4,936 diamonds, or like Napoleon, painted by Jean-Auguste-Dominique Ingres, with the famous Regent Diamond of 140.64 carats set upon the hilt of the sword, up to modern times with the British Crown Jewels, in which

the crown and scepter, adorned with the Koh-i-Nur of 105.60 carats and the First Star of Africa of 530.20 carats, respectively, stand out.

Yet this extraordinary mineral, famous for its qualities, consists of common carbon, a chemical element that only turns into diamond in the bowels of the earth in extreme conditions, under great pressure and very high temperatures. At 120 to 150 kilometers below the earth's surface, in the natural cradle known as the mantle, diamond, with other minerals, falls within the range of the deepest existing rocks. Formed over millions of years and destined to run out, just like petroleum, it can melt, liquefy into other minerals, or give birth to rare, unique stones.

Every year, millions of carats of diamonds are extracted from the heart of the earth, riverbeds, or the seabed, but only some can be defined as "fancy diamonds." Marked by extraordinary hues or shades, fancy diamonds are created by the combination of atoms of elements other than carbon. Inside their structure, some atoms of nitrogen or boron can turn yellow or blue diamonds into all the colors of the rainbow. Valued on the basis of the rarity of the color and the lack of inclusions, they are then classified according to a scale of intensity from faint to fancy deep, and their value is decreed by the more or less rare properties of each individual diamond. Among the most renowned fancy diamonds for history and features include pink diamonds, like the Hortensia of 21.32 carats, from the name of Hortense de Beauharnais, Queen of Holland, or the Pink Dream of 59.60 carats, sold at auction at Sotheby's, Geneva, for $83 million in November 2013, making it a world record for the sale of a jewel. Then there are blue diamonds, like the historic French Blue of 45.52 carats, taken to France by Jean Baptiste Tavernier, passed to the French Royal Treasury, subsequently renamed the Hope Diamond, belonged to Evalyn Walsh McLean, and is now in the Smithsonian National Museum of Natural History. And there are green diamonds, including the Dresden Green of 40.72 carats, and yellow diamonds, like the famous Golden Jubilee of 545.67 carats, which is part of the royal treasure of Thailand.

Destined to come to the surface inside rocks of kimberlite, through volcanic eruptions, or in alluvial deposits, the diamond that strikes and fascinates the collective imagination is still, however, the colorless one; in other words, a perfect diamond, one made of only carbon. After the extraction of the rough diamond, according to the type of deposit, mainly in open-cast mines, the material takes the guise of the most elegant geometric forms through the skillful work of cutters, who have passed on the art and secrets of the most celebrated diamonds in the world for generations.

The cutting and cleaning operations highlight the beauty of the diamond by drawing out the fire; i.e., the total internal reflection. All this requires time and research. This stage is very delicate and difficult, as the slightest miscalculation can lead to the loss of substantial sums of money. There is no certain dating that identifies the beginning of the cutter's art, but the first examples take us to India and the route of the treasure of St. Mark's in Venice. Since then, the tools, techniques, and cuts have slowly developed over the centuries—mainly in Antwerp—down to modern times, when the most frequent choice for the diamond remains that known as "brilliant," identifying a round cut with a minimum of fifty-seven or fifty-eight facets. The great diffusion of the brilliant cut has led the public to identify the term "brilliant" with "diamond," even though there are actually various types and forms of diamonds.

The style of the cut as we know it today began with the discovery of huge Indian deposits in the fourteenth century and the all-Italian idea of using diamond dust to polish and harmonize the surfaces of the crystal in nature. This was followed by the invention of the table and rose cuts, arriving into the seventeenth century, when we had news of the gems imported from India through the French merchant Jean Baptiste Tavernier. At this time the Mazarin cut and its variants flourished, moving into the eighteenth century with the Old Mine cut.

Like a picture or a sculpture, the cut is also a work of art, particularly for the larger stones, where the work is still partly manual. In addition to the brilliant cut—the best known—handed-down cuts include the Pear, Oval, Marquise, Emerald, and Heart cuts and various other "fancy" cuts, including the recent Princess, Radiant, and Barion cuts. Through the cut, the stone is transformed into a gem and is classified on the basis of the four Cs: cut, color, clarity, and carat. That is, its value is determined by the type of cut and the proportions adopted, the analysis for the absence of color, the study for any imperfections (called inclusions), and, lastly, an estimate of the weight.

The absence of color is assessed according to an international scale developed and promoted by the Gemological Institute of America since 1973—from D, colorless, for the whitest gems, through to Z, shade by shade, for the most intense gradations of yellow and fancy diamonds.

The analysis of purity is measured and assessed on the basis of an enlargement of ten times the stone in order to ascertain the size and location of any internal imperfections, such as inclusions of graphite, sulfur, or another substance. The levels of classification highlight the stones free of internal or external inclusions with the FL (Flawless) graph and the various stages follow one another, up to level I3 (Included 3), where the imperfections are clearly visible to the naked eye and reduce the return in the brilliance of the stone to the point of compromising the structure and making it more fragile.

The weight of the diamond has been expressed in carats since ancient times. The term derives from carob seeds, which, according to an old Indian belief, were thought to all be of equal weight. In 1832, the weight of precious stones in carats was precisely defined as the equivalent of 0.20 grams. Only one diamond in a million weighs more than a carat.

After this long path, this beautiful mineral, extracted, cut, weighed, and estimated, is presented to the public, transformed into a gem and, after a millennium, still fascinates people with its infinite properties. In the beginning, the deposits of the most beautiful stones in the world were in India, then Brazil, but South Africa remains in the collective imagination both for the discovery of diamonds, such as the Cullinan, Star of South Africa; Excelsior; Jonker; Centenary and various others, and also for the famous mine in Kimberley, the so-called Big Hole. Since 1924, Damiani has carefully selected the gems to set in its diamond creations according to the criteria of the four Cs from among these wonders of nature. It has distinguished itself for almost a century as the ambassador of a family tradition, combined with a deep passion for entrepreneurial art.

In addition to a taste for luxury, design, and careful workmanship, Damiani pays special attention to ethics, in particular choosing to work only with companies certificated by the World Diamond Council to combat the illegal trade of "blood diamonds," or "conflict diamonds." By becoming a member of the Kimberley Process, the international agreement that ensures that the revenue from the diamond trade is not used to finance civil wars, the company has made an important choice: to contribute to the creation of a partial stabilization of the political situation in some African countries, promoting their economic development and encouraging growth and the respect for human rights. The decision to fight violence and corruption by adhering to the Kimberley Process demonstrates how this market leader wanted to add a deep sense of ethics to the work, in addition to embracing the creativity and innovation in the field of Italian jewelry.

edited by

SARA MICONI

Jewelry Specialist Deputy Director Sotheby's

When the craftsmen say it can't be done, that's the time to insist.

GIORGIO GRASSI DAMIANI

LABORIOUS HANDS

Valenza is a town of workshops. Small goldsmith workshops prosper in anonymous buildings without signs. Damiani stands out. At Via del Lavoro 6, the factory of the group is a square white building with essential architecture on which the gigantic Damiani logo stands. About one hundred people are employed in the various departments—modeling and CAD drawing, preparation of the wax and casting, the goldsmith, selection of the gemstones and raw materials, setting, cleaning, galvanism, and quality control. There is passionate research into design at the source of each creation, conducted by the team of designers working in the offices in Valenza. Every piece of jewelry is the result of in-depth technical and gemological knowledge and refined craftsman expertise. However, before this, it is the recollection of the experience acquired over time and the elaborate projects that mark the history of the brand, which identifies the special creative style. Damiani loves to define its craftsmanship to stress the manual nature of each stage of the processing. The production process starts with the creation of the prototype on the basis of a freehand drawing, which is sometimes perspective in two dimensions and sometimes is just a pen or pencil sketch.

The design is produced in 3-D by the CAD designers who create precise models, giving a virtual shape to the design on paper using prototyping machines with specific programs. The development of the production starts with the mold of the prototype, which can be in brass, wax, or resin. After a careful check on operation, the rubbers are numbered, cataloged, and archived in the wax department, where liquid wax–injection machines, under vacuum—with which the waxes needed for production are created—are used here.

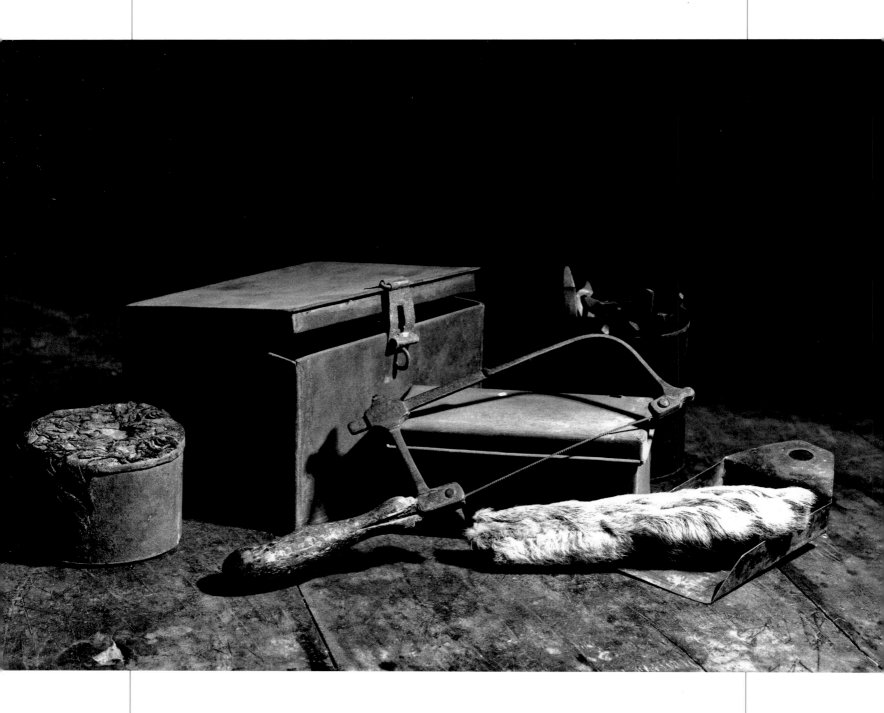

Goldsmiths' tools

Assembled by order and quantity, they are then mounted on the so-called "tree," a rubber base from which a trunk with various branches rises and the waxes are fixed to the ends. The next stage is lost-wax precision casting. After coating the tree with plaster for casting, the wax encased in the plaster is heated and melted, to fill any empty forms. After cooling, the next step is from the casting workshop to the workbench. Once casted, the products are collected and cataloged by order and distributed to the goldsmiths, who have the task of finishing the object with traditional soldering methods. All the creations are stamped and hall-marked on the bench to indicate the manufacture, the titer of the alloy, and the identification mark. The assembled jewelry then passes to the hands of the cleaners and then subjected to quality control, which is carried out at each stage of the process.

In the setting department, the precious stones and diamonds are meticulously analyzed and selected before setting. In addition to diamonds, the symbol of Damiani jewelry, the most frequently used gems are sapphires, rubies, emeralds, aquamarines, onyxes, amethysts, quartzes, turquoises, and then pearls—white, black, and pink. Finally, the last stage involves rhodium plating, which is carried out on jewelry in white gold or platinum. A bath, which coats the surface of the metal with a very thin layer of rhodium, increases the brightness and shine of white gold and platinum. Every gesture of the skilled craftsmen hides jealously guarded secrets, acquired with experience, that result in exclusive creations whose value lies in the unique-ness of the workmanship, where the value is given not only by the variety and cut of the gems but also, and above all, by a rare manual skill, cultivated with a passion that shines through in every elaborate creation and is witnessed by the words of the staff who all feel, in some sense, like its creators.

Perhaps the secret lies in the uniqueness of the Damiani style—not just certificated gems, even in the small carats, with a very high color scale, but an original creativity and a virtuous manufacturing expertise that enables pavé of unique imagination to be produced; complex patterns of mountings draw smooth curves and soft weaves that are difficult to imitate.

All the collections, and particularly the Masterpieces, are the result of a skill in execution that makes pre-cious patterns of mountings possible, similar to fine weaving, with a technique defined by Damiani. Every creation, also if studied inversely, reveals a complex writing of minute settings that relate to a particular stylistic choice and a special executive ability. Although nurtured by profound knowledge of the history of jewelry and an uncommon ability in the choice of gemstones, Damiani collections do not reveal retro reminiscences or analogies with pieces of other brands. Being a part of an original pathway in different roles creates a sentimental identification with the company that becomes a kind of large family, where passion and harmony reign for all those working there.

A special atmosphere can be clearly perceived in the Damiani workshop in Valenza. It captures, almost instinctively, the feeling of cohesive work, a special attention to measured gestures and the love for shared work, for a purpose that is considered as your own, giving the very best of your personal skills. All the staff, in every department, have this attitude, which originates in the pride of being creators of the collections of a successful brand that is able to stand out internationally through their own creations. The Damianis are able to get their staff involved and make them feel like an integral part of the company and the creative processes; feel like part of a family that works harmoniously, with the understanding that they each will support one another. Visiting the workshop and talking to employees, each piece of jewelry seems to be a "creature," bred through the different experiences of all the staff, partly crafted by each but of which every-one knows the genesis to perfection, almost as though it had been created by just one pair of hands. The master goldsmiths confess that they feel a special satisfaction in explaining jewelry, because talking about it allows them to transmit the acquired skill. They recall the genesis of exclusive creations in the numbering of the details, the cut of the gemstones, their brilliance—enhanced by the special settings and the elaborate pavé—and savor the pride of being part of a special alchemy. A design takes shape, like a mosaic, from the composition of the gems, a precious material that needs to be learned to know, educating the eye with daily observation.

All Damiani production is created in the area of Valenza. Of this, most is made in the workshop of the group at Via del Lavoro, 6. It's no coincidence that there is a square dedicated to Damiano Grassi Damiani in Valenza, which faces the company's offices. In the center of the square, there is a fountain with water gushing from a large *D*. Damiani is a just source of pride, not only for Valenza, but for the whole of Italy, with 100 percent of the production made in Italy, and who has been able to construct a unique, distinguish-able style in the contemporary jewelry design.

DESIGNING JEWELRY WITH PASSION

Behind every Damiani creation there is the skill of selecting gemstones, which depends on a network of reliable suppliers, built up over time as a result of the brand's prestige and the charisma of the Damiani siblings, who invest their talent in serving the group with creative and strategic ideas that are always new, and a team of designers recruited from jewelry design schools, particularly through the Advanced Training Course in Jewelry Design of the Politecnico di Milano, with which Damiani has a consolidated partnership relationship.

More than artists, Damiani's creative team feel as if they are designers, or lovers engaged in technical challenges. Jewelry, unlike other arts, requires precious raw materials. The desire to dare, to tackle projects with the limits of feasibility, is a continuous challenge that brings growth in creativity, technical ability, aesthetics, and quality of execution. Following the creative process in Damiani, numerous analogies between jewelry and haute couture emerge. "The paper cutouts are obtained from the drawings," says one of the designers. "For some pieces, a paper model is also created, and tests are carried out; for example, for the ring that covers the whole finger, which is custom-made for the customer, or for certain high necklaces, which need to be made according to the neck size."

A piece of jewelry is like a dress; it has to be worn. The difference is in the materials, unmistakably more precious. Fit and feel are very important. At Damiani, they are convinced that jewelry must make the wearer dream and that the best experience is seeing the shining eyes of a customer wearing one of their pieces.

The Masterpieces are made to transmit craftsman virtuosity. Medusa is an example of Damiani excellence. It is a necklace that caresses the neck; soft as velvet, fully jointed, moving fluidly like a jellyfish in water. The inspiration for the Masterpieces doesn't only come from the world of jewelry and its tradition, but also from nature, music, architecture, art, poetry, stories, and more. All this is translated according to technical and aesthetic rules, with great respect for the precious materials that are used, and because of the experience of those assembling them, something unique and rare is created that will remain over time.

Jewelry serves to make a woman more beautiful, but it also has a more profound meaning: it represents an emotion, a desire, or a memory. It's no accident that the etymology refers to the word "joy."

In a world where everything needs a reason for being, jewelry lives its own life. It has the value, taste, and emotion of what only exclusively exists to be beautiful and to adorn the person who desires it. Men and women have always felt the desire to bedeck themselves to show power, social role, and wealth; the need to take care of the details, and respect the meaning and importance of something that may seem superfluous but which embodies archaic meanings that have always accompanied mankind.

All too often, jewelry has only been considered as an investment, but its true value, above all, lies in what it means for those who give and receive it.

There is a history and culture of jewelry in every country, and common origins can often be found. The signs that come from afar, and the past, can be reinvented with the intention of reaching out to the heart and soul of the person who will wear it.

In designing the Damiani collections, the creative team always considers the relationship between freedom of expression and the need to adapt to a style identifiable now, in addition to the importance of dealing with the market. The beauty of a piece often depends on the balance, proportions, and subtle details that may seem like an unnecessary virtuosity but make the difference in jewelry, which always works on minimum dimensions and with very costly raw materials.

The intention is to think of iconic products that express luxury but are soft, fresh, and accessible to wear every day. Finding the balance between invention, style of the brand, and ability to respond to the needs of the market, and creating a product for a broader clientele, is perhaps more difficult than designing a unique piece. In this, Damiani is an exemplary case in the world of jewelry and is, to all effects, a design company.

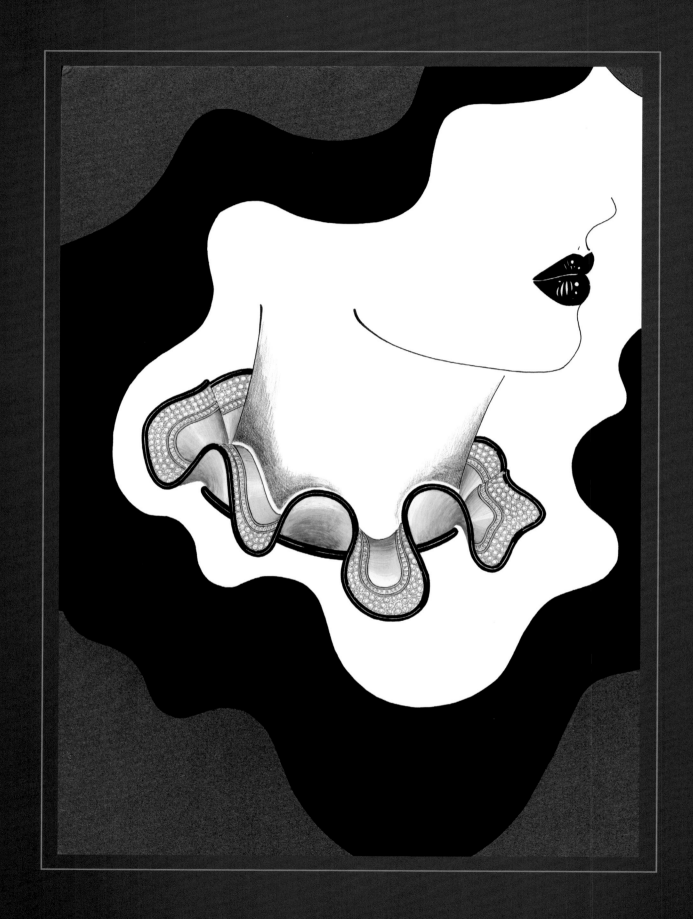

The
Diamonds
International
Awards

The Diamonds International Awards paid homage to the most original and important designs created in fine jewelry for almost fifty years. Considered the Academy Awards of the industry, they are the most influential and prestigious recognition for jewelry design, honoring the best creations using diamonds. Receiving one of these awards is the highest recognition that a jewelry company can aspire to, and Damiani is the only one to have won eighteen of them–an unbeaten record.

Shark

DIAMOND INTERNATIONAL AWARD 1976

Created in platinum and yellow gold, this bracelet, designed by Gabriella Grassi Damiani, is fully illuminated by a pavé of white diamonds and absolutely pure *jonquilles* for a total of 41.19 carats, with an original self-locking clip that elegantly encircles the arm.

Bloody Mary

DIAMOND INTERNATIONAL AWARD 1986

Mary Tudor inspired this regal collier, which recalls the ancient collars of princely clothes. The woven effect is achieved through the chromatic variation of the burnished gold and yellow gold and the setting of 1,121 brilliant- and baguette-cut diamonds weighing an overall 87.98 carats. A demanding workmanship shaped the gold in a form of waves into which the gems are set. The final outcome is of stupefying elasticity, sitting naturally on the neck, as if Bloody Mary was nothing other than the work of an imaginative tailor when, instead, it is the result of a highly sophisticated technique that engaged the best master jewelers and setters for twelve months.

Vulcano

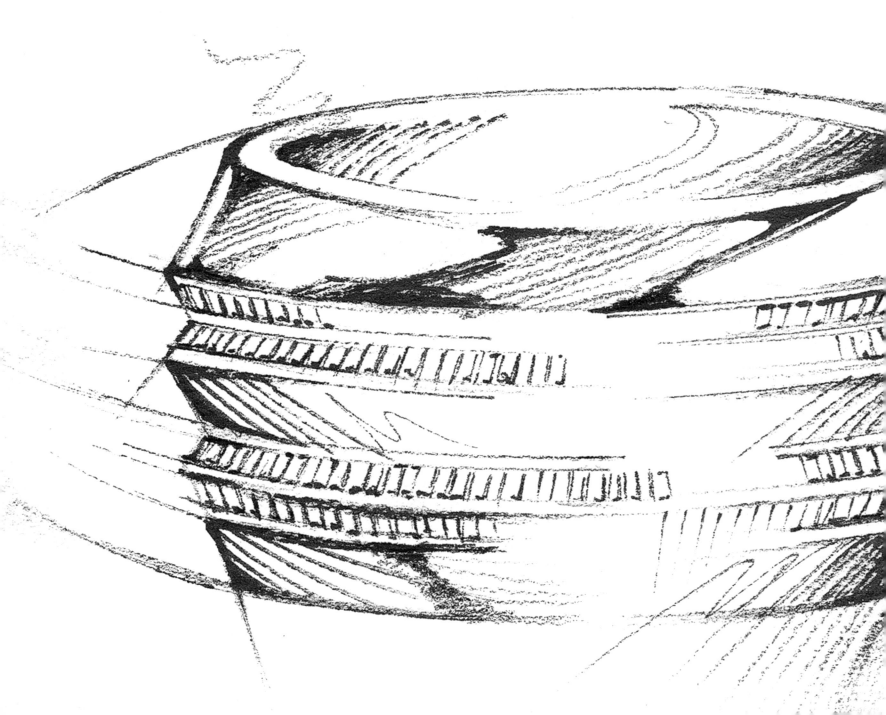

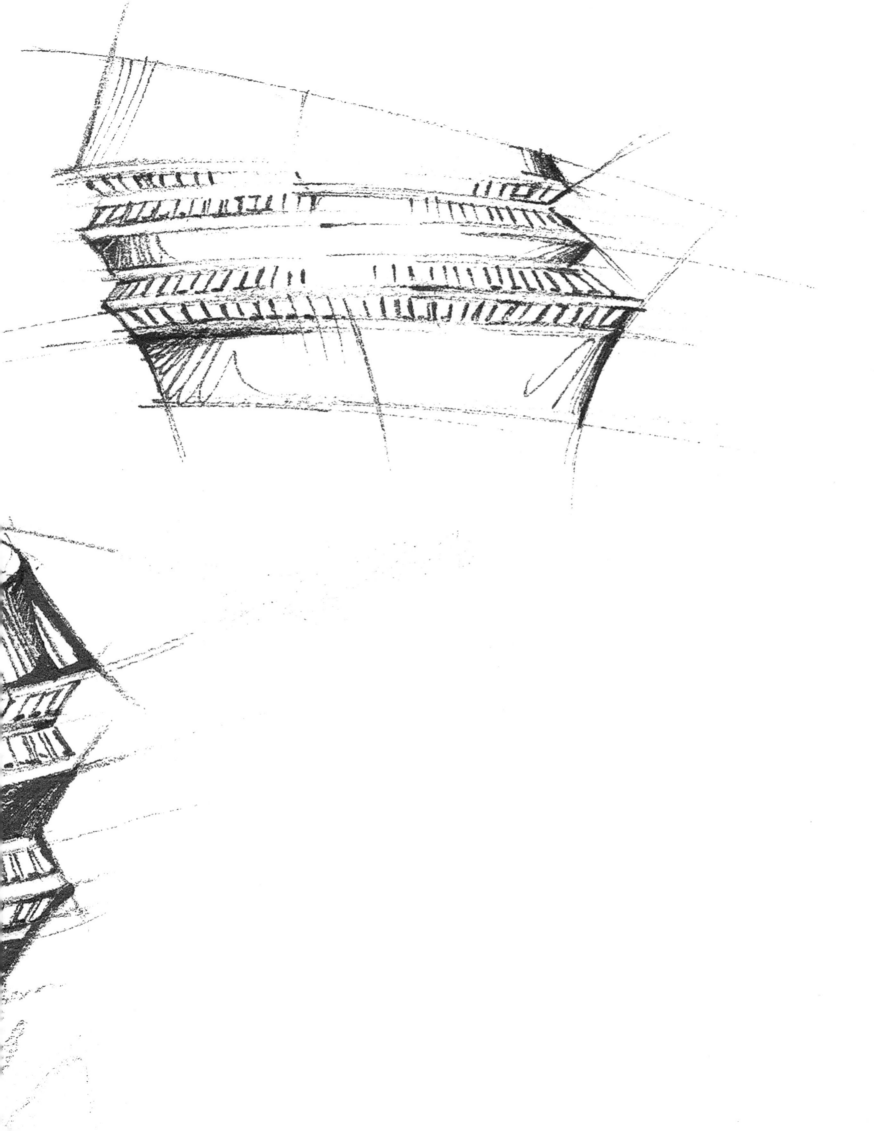

Vulcano

DIAMOND INTERNATIONAL AWARD 1988

The essentiality and purity of the design are the main features of this bracelet. The contrast between an intentionally strong design and the smooth finish of the gold recall the origins of the creative act, as though it was a mediation between primordial nature and sophisticated art. The task of valorizing the structure of the jewel, created with 185.70 grams of gold, is entrusted to 346 baguette-cut diamonds, for an overall 40.63 carats that create surfaces of intense light.

spaziale

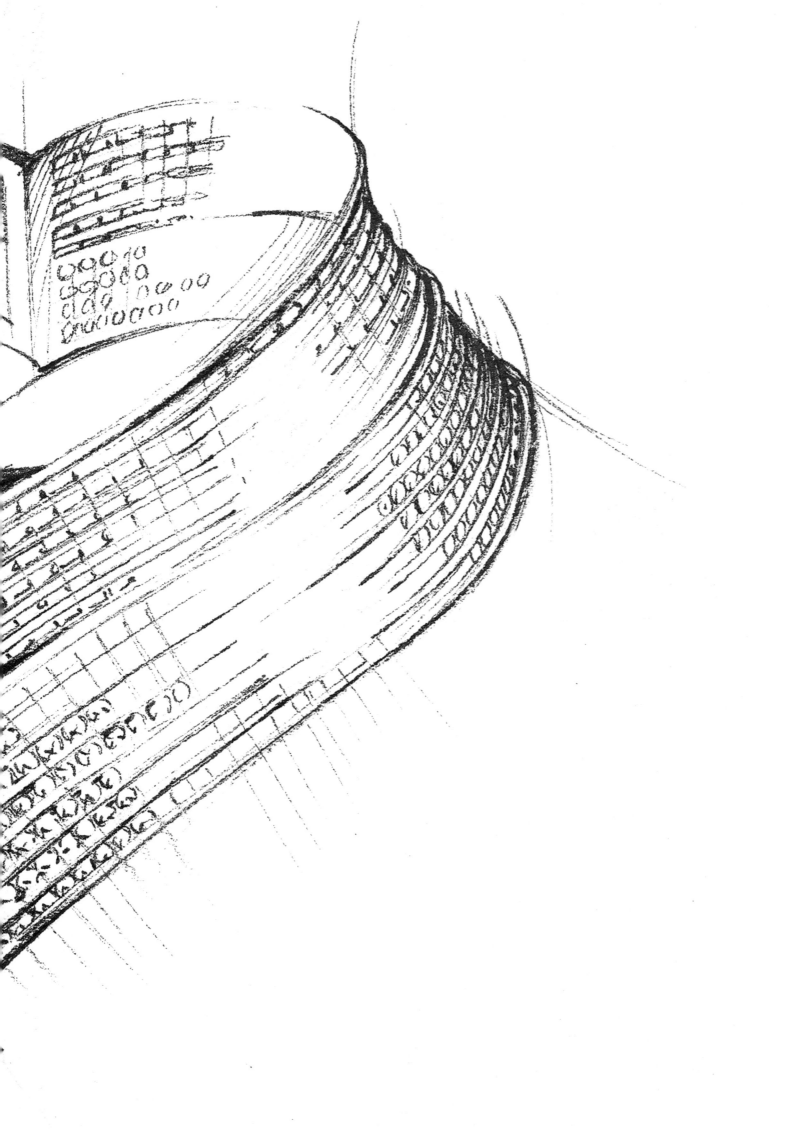

Spaziale

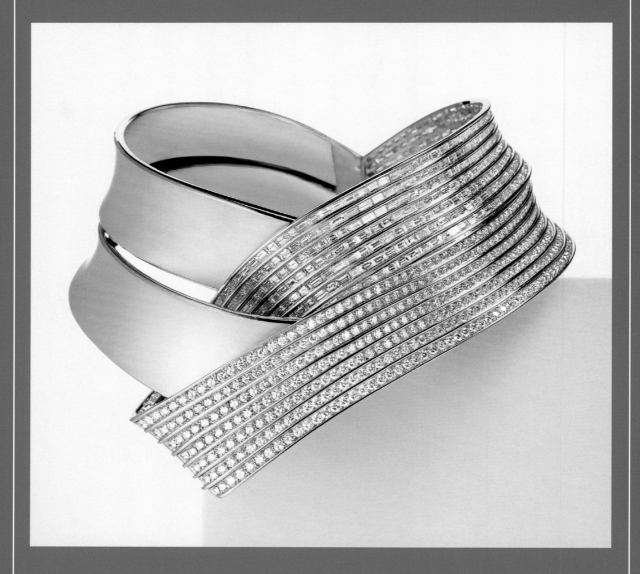

DIAMOND INTERNATIONAL AWARD 1988

This necklace is distinguished by the contrast of the materials and the avant-garde purity of the lines. The swing-away bands are in satin-finish platinum and yellow gold, studded with 646 brilliant-cut diamonds and 476 baguette-cut diamonds totaling 127.68 carats. The solution adopted for the closure is innovative, giving comfort and satisfaction to the wearer, as the rigid, solid collier opens in two.

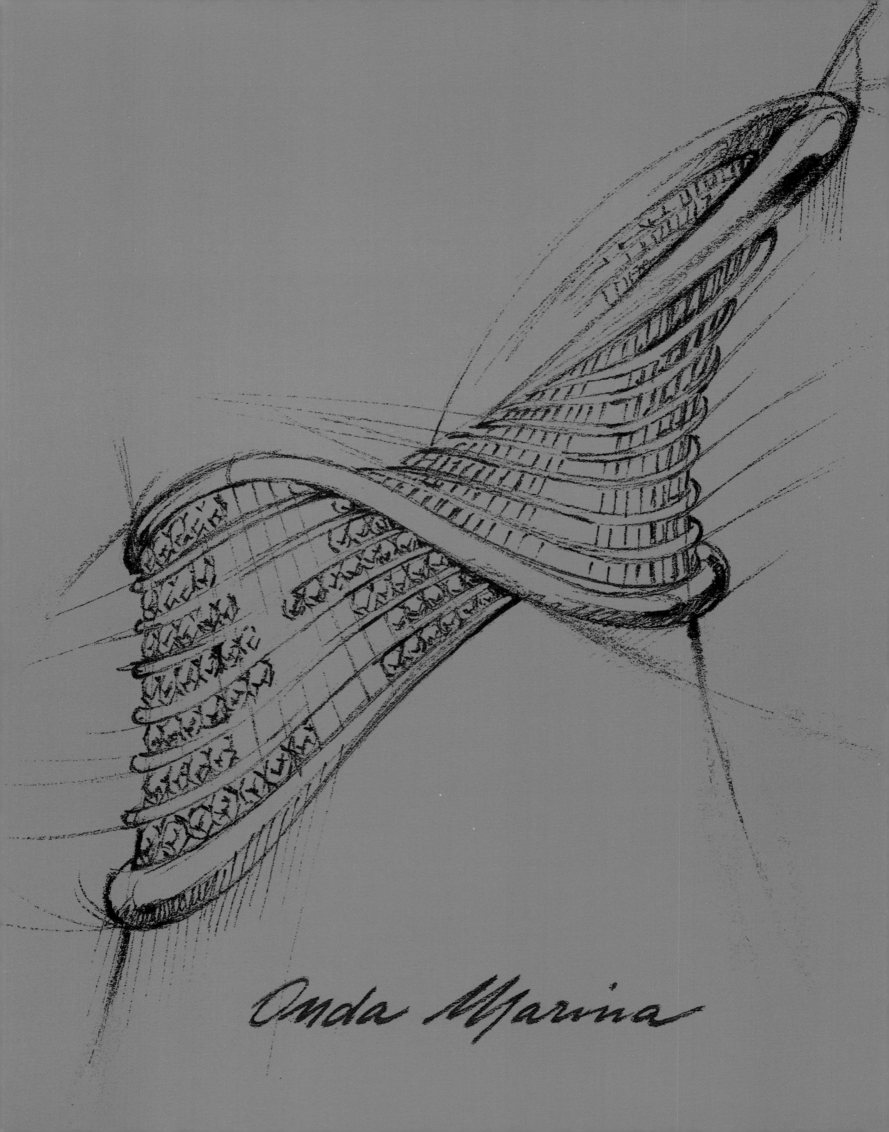

Onda Marina

Onda Marina

DIAMOND INTERNATIONAL AWARD 1988

Bubbling with light and harmonious in movement, this bracelet is a precious wave that unfolds in elegant spirals. Illuminated by 644 brilliant and baguette diamonds totaling 46.21 carats, Onda Marina achieves a spectacular material effect.

Piovra

DIAMOND INTERNATIONAL AWARD 1990

Free creative imagination gave life to this original, unexpected, and unparalleled bracelet. The stunning design is enhanced by an extraordinary number of diamonds: 958 pure gems totaling 80.63 carats. In platinum and yellow gold, Piovra recalls the mysterious charm of the deep sea with its variously undulating surfaces that play with the lines of the metal, the light of the diamonds, and the shadows of the slate, an unusual material in jewelry.

Chignon

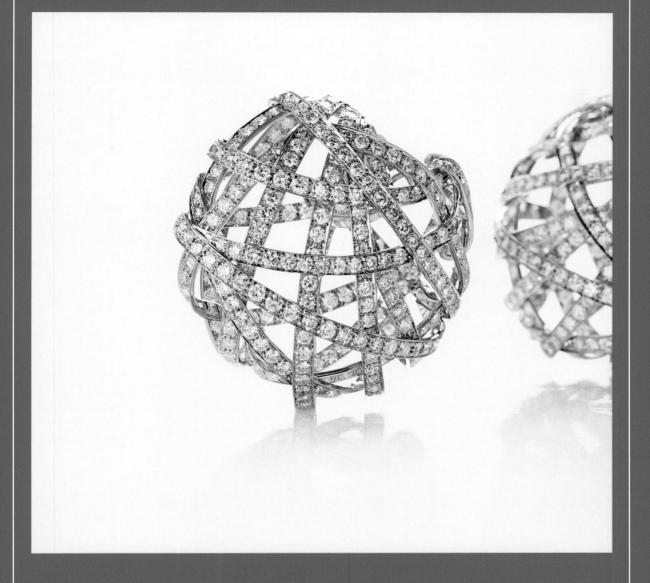

DIAMOND INTERNATIONAL AWARD 1994

A tangle of platinum, red gold, and yellow gold tapes in a chromatic game illuminated by the white light of 280 diamonds. With the harmony of the spheres skillfully constructed on the alternation of solids and spaces, these earrings are the result of highly refined jewelry craftsmanship whose precious weave is lightly forged like lace.

Hong Kong Lights

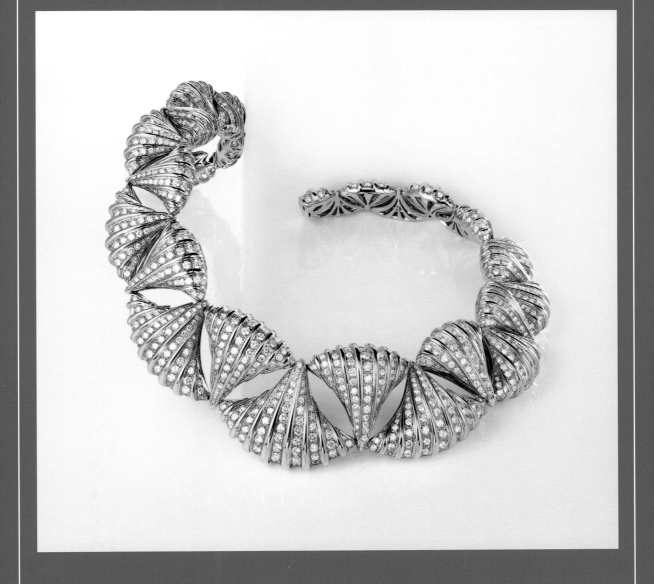

DIAMOND INTERNATIONAL AWARD 1994

This necklace, designed by Giorgio Grassi Damiani, consists of a series of slightly bombé triangular elements, alternating platinum, yellow, and red gold on which 1,450 round, brilliant-cut diamonds are aligned for a total of 59.56 carats. A collier of sophisticated architecture and extraordinary light.

Sahara

DIAMOND INTERNATIONAL AWARD 1996

Sahara is a unique bracelet, inspired by the movement of the rippling dunes and the dazzling light of infinite mirages. Suggesting the impalpable movements of the desert with white gold requires refined goldsmith ability, while entrusting the magic of unreal contours to the light of 1,865 diamonds requires elevated gemological sensitivity and knowledge of the best setting techniques. Sahara is creative imagination of the goldsmiths' art and gemological quality.

Blue Moon

DIAMOND INTERNATIONAL AWARD 1996

The half moon, a very old jewelry motif and dream symbol par excellence, is the inspiration for these earrings, which are dedicated to dreams. The part in yellow gold represents the lunar profile upon which sparkle 13.9 carats of diamonds set in white gold, which seem suspended in space. Their layout is only apparently irregular, but in reality positions on different levels has been developed to create an image of chiaroscuro evoking the spots on the moon and suggesting an imaginary sense of depth. The particular closure of the earrings continues the motif into the rear of the lobe, producing an illusory effect that seems to challenge the laws of physics.

Twins

DIAMOND INTERNATIONAL AWARD 1996

A spectacular ring in yellow gold, undulating with a double band of 118 pure baguette-cut diamonds for a total of seven carats. The particularity of this ring is its three-dimensional aspect, which also illustrates the setting of the diamonds in the side thickness of the jewel and underlines the effect of luminous, precious waves.

The Wheel

DIAMOND INTERNATIONAL AWARD 1998

A round bracelet in yellow gold illuminated by 380 baguette-cut diamonds totaling 42 carats. This is an essential and modern design, a decorative motif that recalls a chessboard, alternating gold and diamonds, for a soft, perfect creation.

Eden

DIAMOND INTERNATIONAL AWARD 2000
Seduction, charm, and femininity are the inspirations for Eden, a bracelet that encircles the arm with light and femininity. Created in about 800 hours of work in white gold and 900 brilliant-cut diamonds for a total of 94.45 carats set on eleven elements and the two ends.

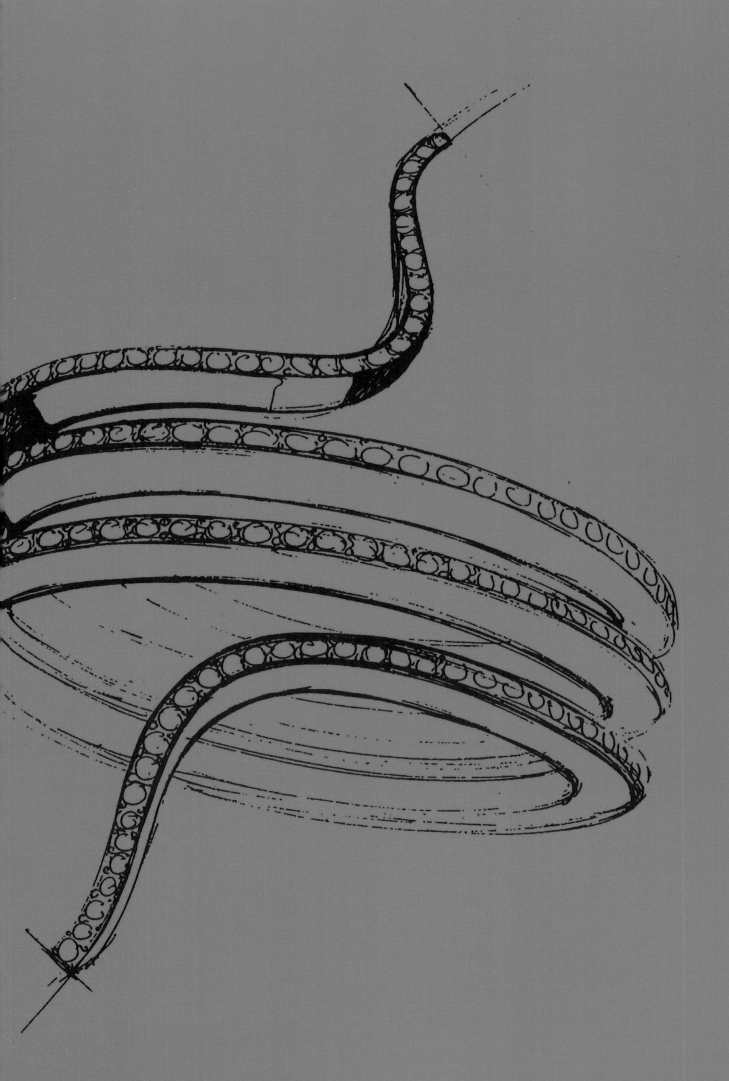

* EDEN EFF. TIMBR°

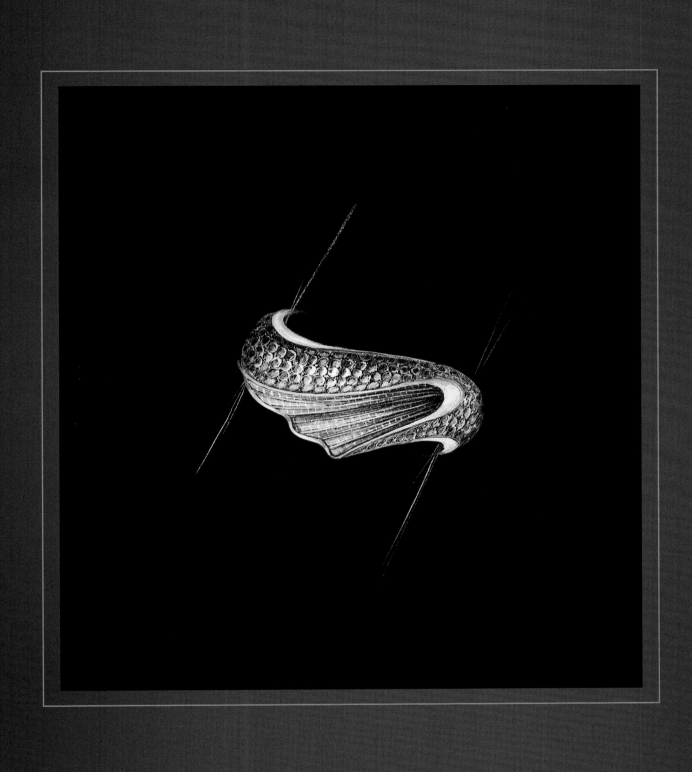

Masterpieces

Masterpieces of the goldsmiths' art, these jewels are exceptional, unique pieces, designed for special occasions, to be worn and to highlight the beauty of the women who choose them.
Every year, Damiani presents its new Masterpieces, extraordinary creations of sophisticated design, fruit of the creativity of Damiani and its team of designers working at the company's jewelry workshop in an itinerant exhibition.
These exclusive, exceptional items are entirely handmade in the Damiani ateliers in Valenza, and they are so much more than *Made in Italy–* they are *Made in Valenza*, the symbolic place for high quality in the world of signature jewelry and for the brands that have made Italy and its luxury products great.

Burlesque

The world of the burlesque is the source of inspiration for this bracelet in white gold and diamonds, inspired by boudoirs and lingerie, corsets and laces. The clasp consists of two chains that cross like the laces in a corset in order to adjust its size. Burlesque is a rigid but jointed bracelet, soft on the wrist, an authentic work of goldsmiths' art.

Sharon Stone and Giorgio Damiani during a press conference

Mediterranea

A beautiful cuff bracelet in white gold with coral *cabochon* surrounded by white diamonds and yellow, light blue, pink, and lilac sapphires, all set by hand at different heights to exalt the light better. A true work of fine jewelry that draws inspiration from the colors and light of the Mediterranean.

Belle Époque

Dedicated to the Belle Époque and its magic atmosphere, these historic Masterpieces take the lines of the first jewels created by Enrico Grassi Damiani. They celebrate a period of great social and cultural growth at the beginning of the twentieth century and represent a valuable tribute to film and the design of its side perforations. Rings, crosses, bracelets, necklaces, tiaras, and watches with full essential lines are created in white gold and diamonds, occasionally alternating with sapphires, rubies, and emeralds.

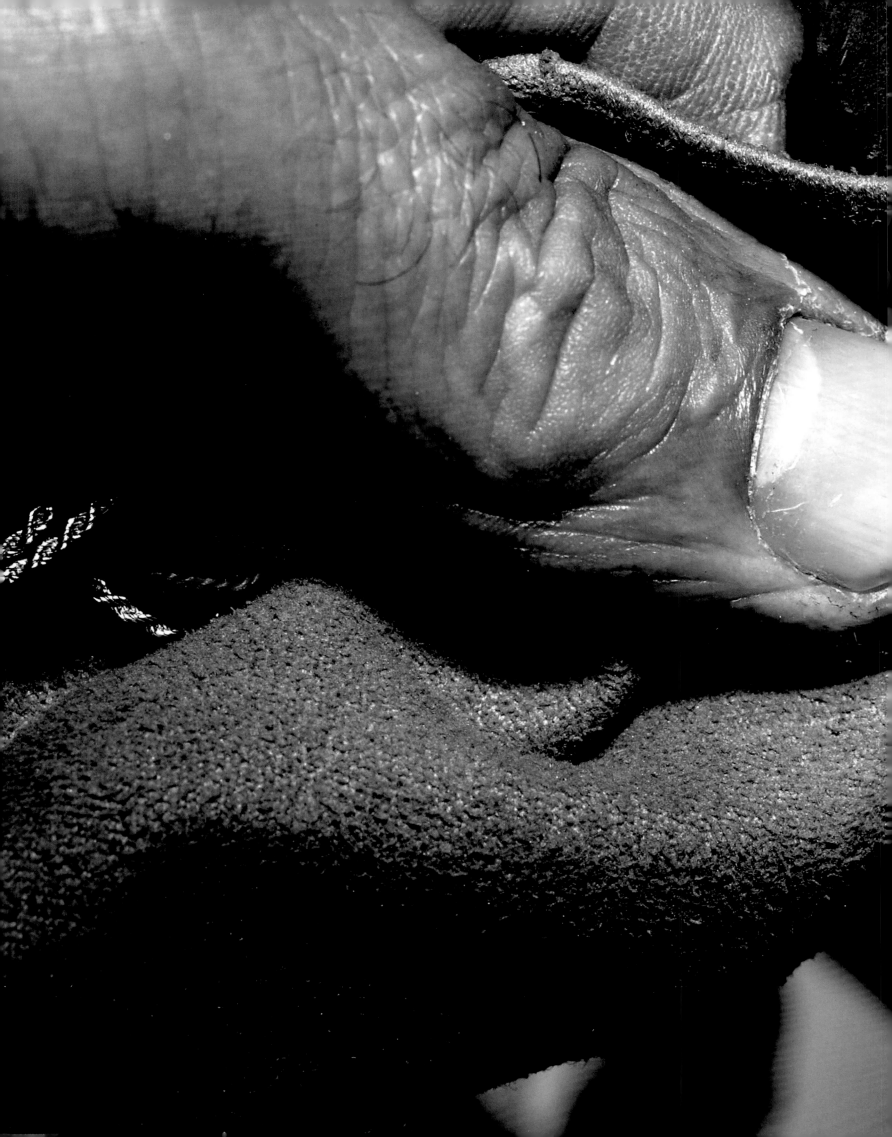

Cincillà

A splendid collier, designed to suggest a neck softly wrapped in fur, created by setting white and iced diamonds on a mounting in burnished gold, with shades from black to gray. The sophisticated burnishing technique, which covers part of the claw, highlights the different degrees of colors and creates an extremely refined final effect, an elegant play of light, shade, and contrast between the brilliance of the different diamonds and gold.

Sharon Stone, 62nd Cannes Festival, 2009

Anima

This explosion of color is achieved through a design that enhances the central stone in a contemporary style using the Damiani setting technique called "apparent chaos," which plays with the effect of the light and the stones set at various levels, according to the color. The combination of gems and different cuts highlights the design and the three-dimensional aspect of this collection of classic inspiration.

Vulcania

·—◆—·

Precious stones, like incandescent lava shimmering in various tones and shades of color. Vulcania is a necklace made with white, fancy, and brown diamonds in an unlimited, sophisticated chromatic variation. An authentic masterpiece of fine jewelry that could only be created through the skills of Damiani's expert master goldsmiths and setters.

I FEEL EXACTLY LIKE A QUEEN BECAUSE INSTEAD OF HAVING A CROWN ON MY HEAD, I HAVE IT AROUND MY NECK.

SOPHIA LOREN

La Scala Theatre, 2004

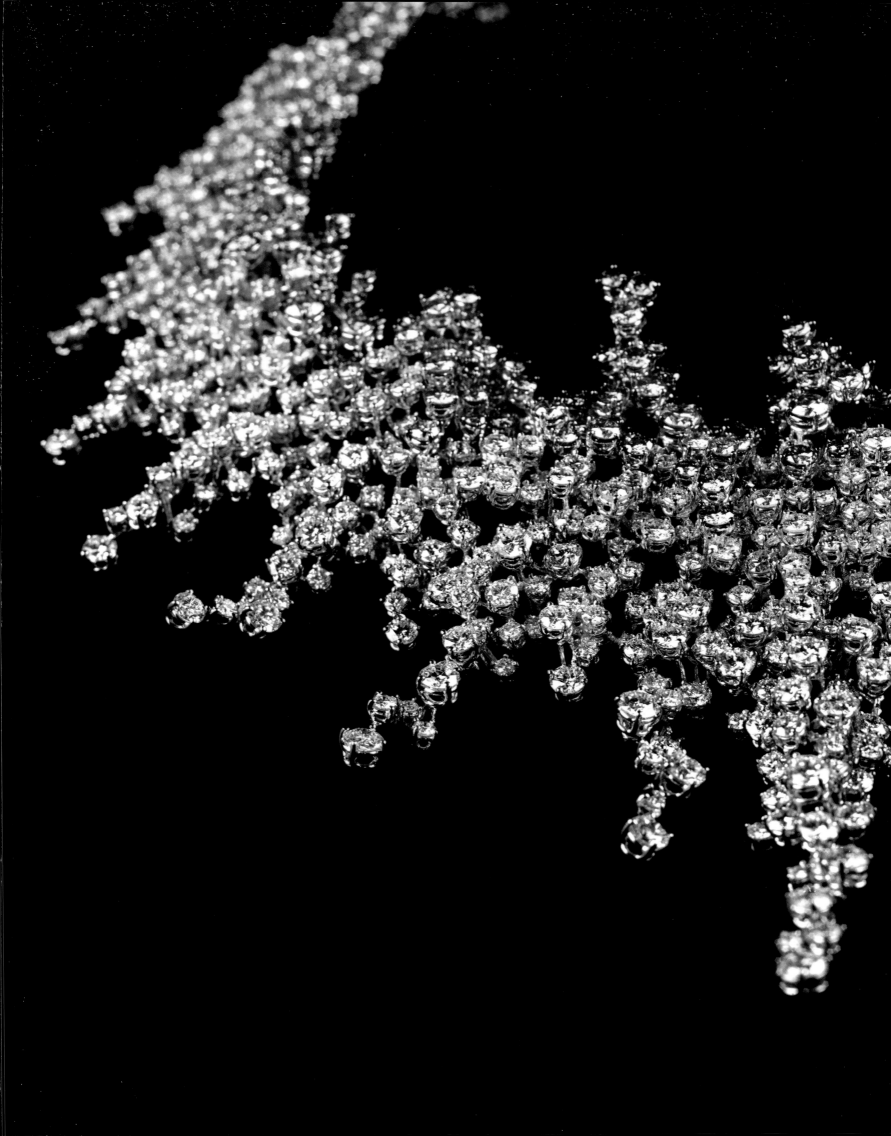

Butterfly

The lightness and delicate flutter of a butterfly's wings are the inspiration for Butterfly. The necklace consists of a sequence of butterflies of different sizes and colors, with the last two central ones being detachable for use as pendants or brooches. With great attention to detail, the quality and lightness of this work are achieved with diamonds and sapphires in colors varying from yellow to orange, pink to red and light to dark blue; the colors of the gemstones have been enhanced by pink, yellow, or brown rhodium plating, all rigorously handmade.

Drip Drops

A linear and essential line that redraws the drop that was an Art Deco jewelry classic. These jewels in gold and gemstones—like diamonds, sapphires of various shades, and aquamarines, carefully selected by expert gemologists—give a highly sophisticated color effect, which makes the pendant and earrings that follow the movements of the neck unique and very light.

DIAMONDS ARE A GIRL'S BEST FRIEND.

MARILYN MONROE

Gentlemen Prefer Blondes, 1953

Juliette

Juliette is an enchanting Masterpiece, where rose-cut diamonds, in use since the fourteenth century in the Netherlands, are united with its special motif—light semicircles, suggestions of the East, architectural details mixing *fin de siècle* atmospheres, Deco rigor, and the lightness of Art Nouveau. These precious jewels, with a mysterious charm, are created in white gold and diamonds as well as emeralds and black diamonds.

Dita Von Teese, 66th Cannes Festival, 2013

Swan

◆

The proud elegance of the swan was the inspiration for the design of Swan. Refined, linear architecture, which recalls the Art Nouveau period, highlights the dark, intense colors of the stones. A cuff bracelet in burnished gold, formed by two wings in pavé of black diamonds, is joined by a completely mobile garnet drop so that it follows the movements of the wrist.

Medusa

The sensual and majestic Medusa necklace is inspired by the obscure submarine world and its creatures, reproducing their shapes and colors. This piece of fine jewelry has a rigid yet soft structure, all in jointed flush-fit claws, and embraces the neck, from which a cascade of precious tentacles of diamonds and sapphires in various shades of light and dark blue, violet, and pink come to life. The working on the underside of the necklace ensures great comfort for the wearer.

Li Bingbing, 64th Cannes Festival, 2011

Notte di San Lorenzo

These jewels are inspired by the beauty and magic of a starry sky and a night of falling stars, that of August 10, feast day of St. Lawrence, Martyr in Italy. This neocontemporary design succeeds in combining the lightness of an essential and modern range and the charm of stones of different sizes, set at different levels, as though they were stars in the sky.

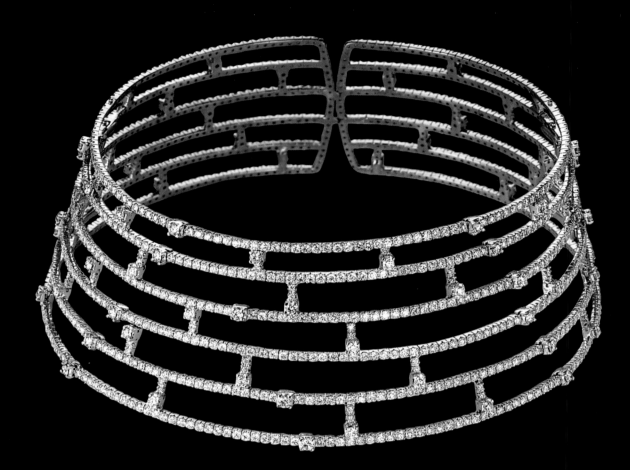

Sharon Stone, Los Angeles, 2009

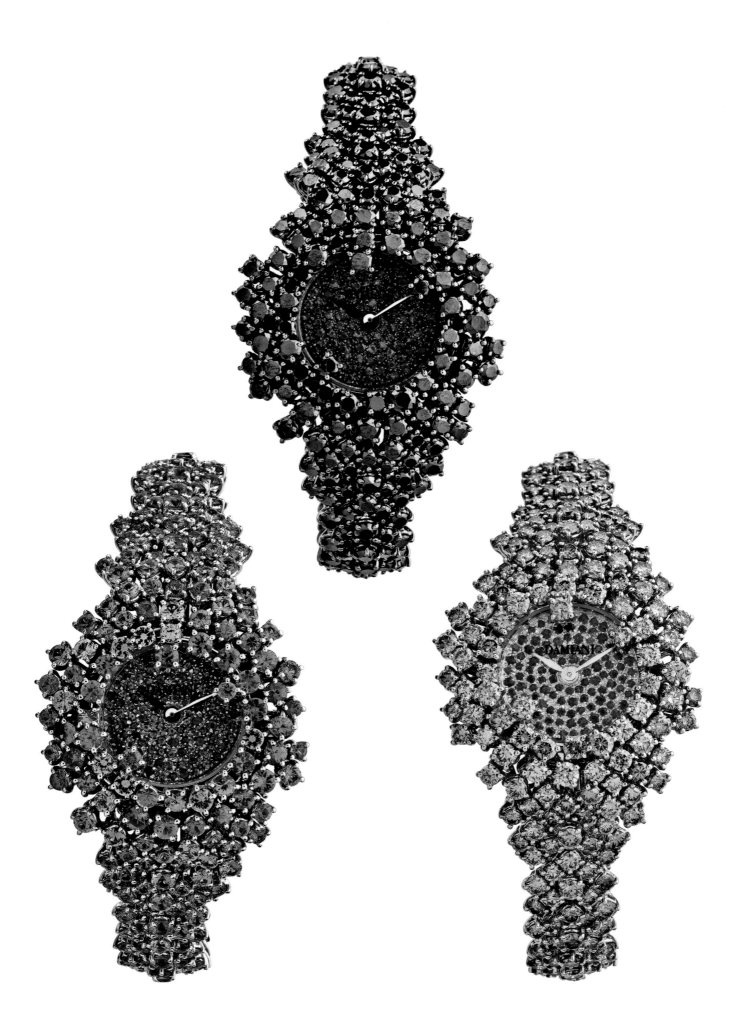

Mimosa

Mimosa watches revolve around a special construction and various shades of color, a combination of precious stones and diamonds that enriches every single watch, like little buds. The gemstones—diamonds, emeralds, rubies, or sapphires—on each case and dial are of different sizes and are set on the bracelet alternately, just like a mimosa flower on a branch. The claw settings are positioned by hand, one by one, by expert master goldsmiths.

Nature

Inspired by nature, Nature shows Damiani's contemporaneity. Precious leaves created in a very light way, using a highly sophisticated technique, enable very fine but highly resistant thicknesses to be worked. The assembly of the various elements is entirely handmade with great aesthetic sensitivity, guaranteeing quality, precision, and balance.

Renaissance

A romantically inspired white gold necklace, made of diamond flowers that enhance the central stone and its intense color—a red ruby, green emerald, or blue sapphire. Renaissance is the modern, sophisticated version of a jewelry classic, where the colored central gemstones are enhanced by the play of light and the alternation of brilliant- and rose-cut diamonds.

Peacock

This spectacular necklace, in white gold with a surprising range of precious stones, is one of the best examples of the skill of Damiani's master goldsmiths. The particular chromatic effect, an explosion of colors that immediately capture the attention, is inspired by the feathers of a peacock, skillfully re-created with the use of diamonds, emeralds, and sapphires.

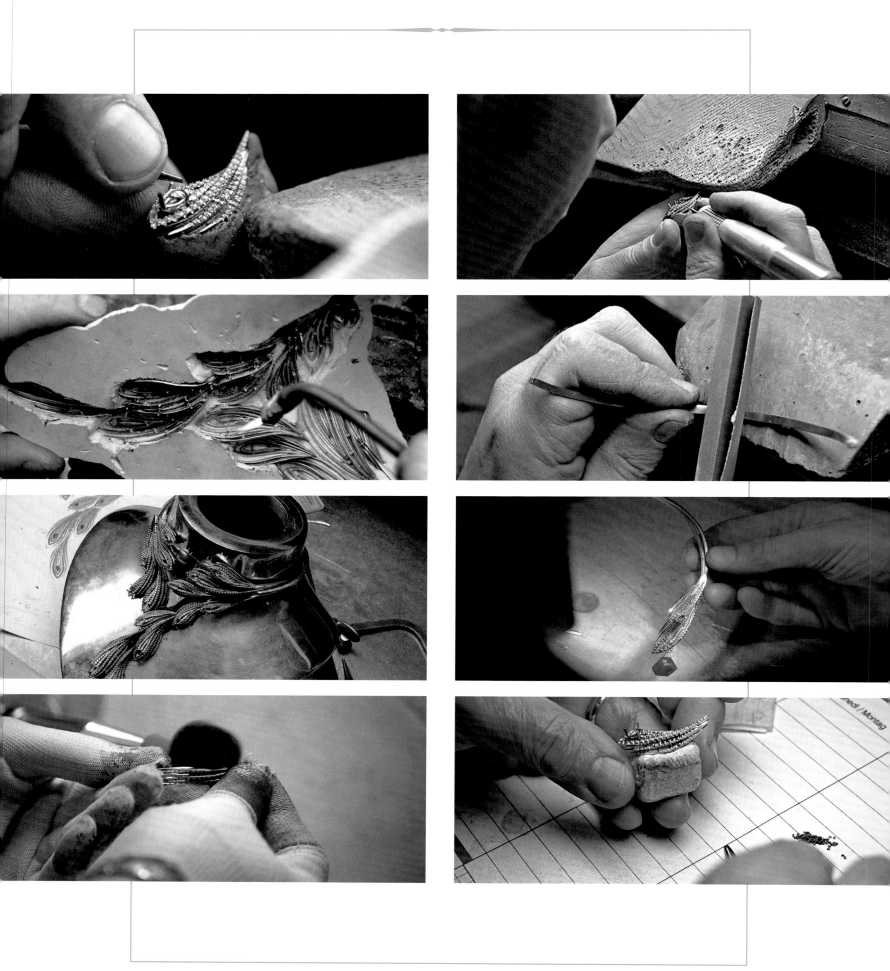

Eden

A soft enveloping spiral in white gold and diamonds that draws inspiration from the Eden bracelet, the eighteenth World Jewelry Oscar won by Damiani in 2000. The bracelet of the Eden watch is entirely handmade, with seven turns in white gold, enriched by 426 diamonds, giving a total of 34.17 carats. Setting these diamonds required more than four days of work by the expert craftsmen in the Damiani workshops.

Nadège du Bospertus, 2002

Vivaldi

The four seasons inspire four rings. Winter plays with the azure of the topazes and the pure white of the diamonds of the chalcedony *cabochon*. A green symphony celebrates spring with tourmalines, peridots, and white diamonds of the green chalcedony *cabochon*. Summer is celebrated by rhodolites, pink sapphires, and white diamonds that surround a cabochon in pink opal. Lastly, autumn aspires to Palmera citrine quartzes, rhodolites, and white diamonds surrounding an orange moonstone *cabochon*.

Printed in April 2014 by EBS - Verona (Italy)